Database Engineer Technique

George W. Jiang

To my lovely and supportive wife, Jing

– George W. Jiang

ACKNOWLEDGMENTS

Thanks to my wonderful wife, Jing who has always supported me in everything. Without her support and encouragement I would not able to match forward in my life and career. I greatly appreciate her patience and understanding during my traveled out from home and spent time on projects.

Thanks also to the teams I worked with on business intelligence projects. Those days and nights with my team members on IT projects had brought me so much precious knowledge and skills that make me able to put notes in this book.

Table of Contents

1. SQL SERVER CLUSTER (PART 1)

This article describes SQL Server 2014 Cluster installation on Windows Server 2012 R2.

SQL Server cluster installation includes the following four parts:

Part 1: Install Windows Server Clustering Service

Part 2: Install SQL Server Cluster on the primary node (WIN_Server1)

Part 3: Install SQL Server Cluster on the secondary node (WIN_Server2)

Part 4: Add SQL Server Agent in cluster resource (option)

Prerequisites

Before performing the installation of SQL Server failover cluster, the following items and permissions are required:

(1) Two dedicated IP addresses.

One IP address is for Windows Server Cluster and other IP address is for SQL Server Cluster.

(2) .NET Framework 3.5 SP1 is a prerequisite.

(3) Windows PowerShell 2.0 is a prerequisite.

(4) Requires administrative permissions on the servers that will become cluster nodes. Also requires Create Computer objects and Read All Properties permissions in the container that is used for computer accounts in the domain.

(5) When the Create Cluster wizard is run, it creates the cluster name account in the default container that is used for computer accounts in the domain. If you create the cluster name account (cluster name object) before creating the cluster, you must give it the Create Computer objects and Read All Properties permissions in the container that is used for computer accounts in the domain.

(6) Installation items listed as examples here:

Two Windows 2012 R2 Servers:

WIN_Server1.Aleafboat.net (192.168.10.7)

WIN_Server2.Aleafboat.net (192.168.10.8)

Windows Cluster instance name: WIN_Cluster

(192.168.10.11)

SQL Server Cluster instance name: SQL_Cluster

(192.168.10.12)

Network: 192.168.10.0/24

Part 1 – Install Windows Server Clustering Service

(1) SQL Server clustering service is based on Windows Server clustering service. It is required to add Windows feature: Failover Clustering.

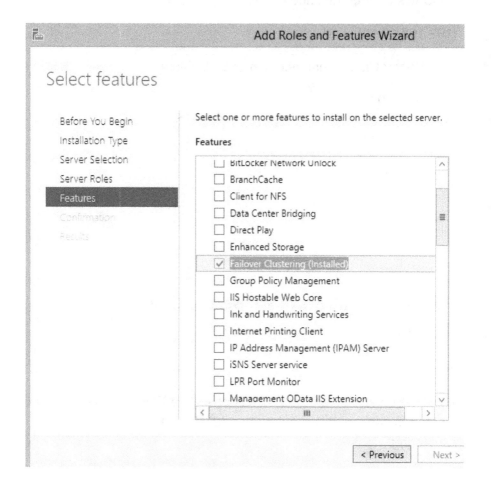

(2) After the new feature is added on server, reboot
Windows server.

(3) From Failover Cluster Manager to validate Windows
Cluster Configuration.

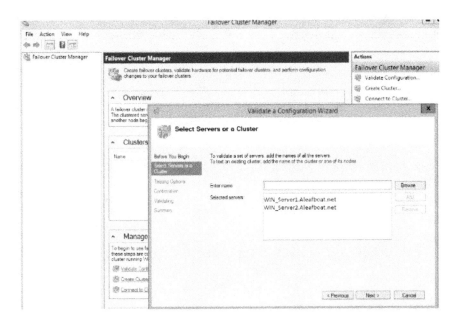

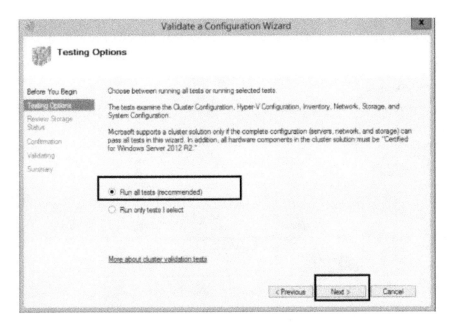

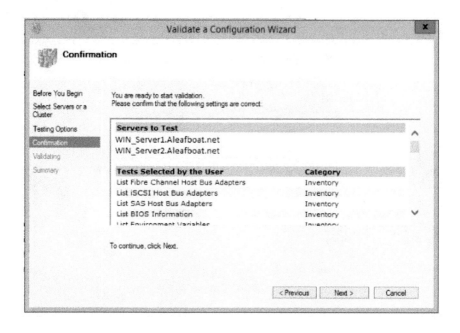

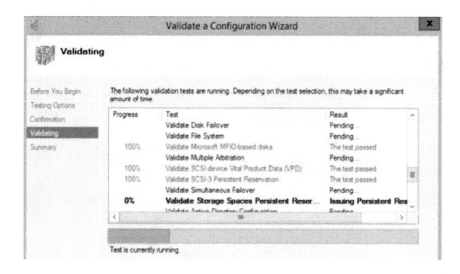

(4) Review validation report:

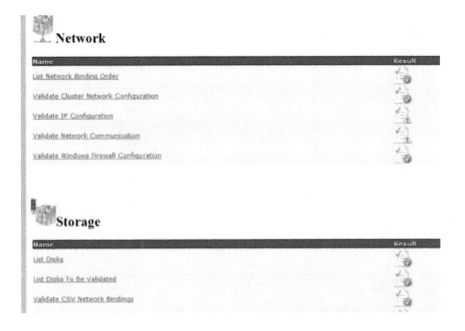

(5) If cluster validation is successful, continuing to create Windows Failover Cluster.

The new Windows Cluster instance name: WIN_Cluster

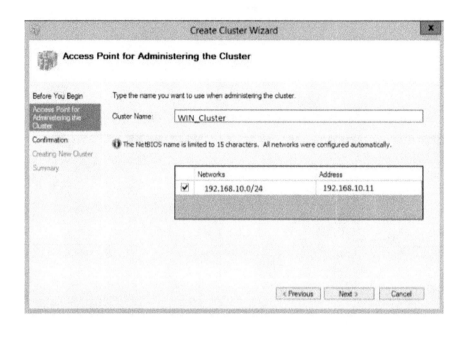

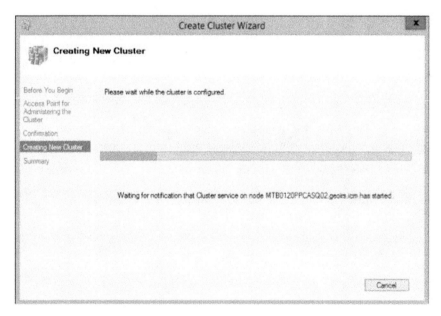

(6) After new Windows Cluster created, verify the new Windows cluster online status:

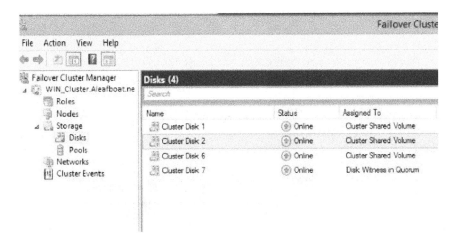

Windows cluster instance WIN_Cluster is available and all cluster disks are online.

Part 1 installation is completed.

Continue to SQL Server cluster installation **Part 2** installation.

2. SQL SERVER CLUSTER (PART 2)

This part describes installation of SQL Server Cluster on the primary node (**WIN_Server1**)

(1) Choose New SQL Server Failover Cluster Installation option to start installation

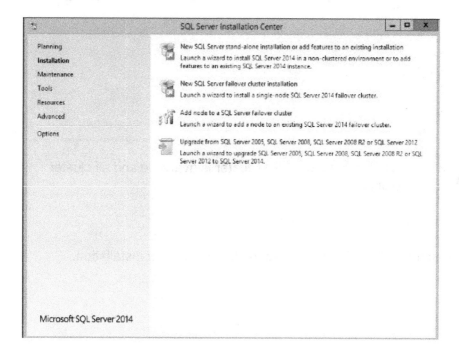

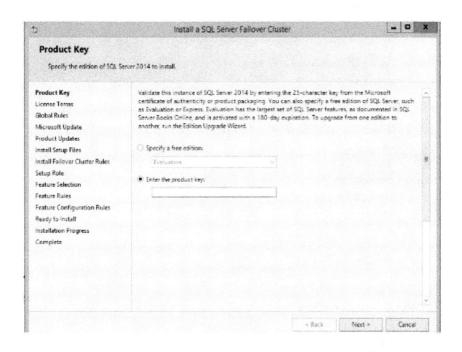

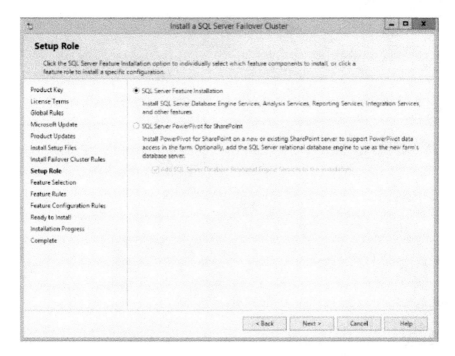

(2) Choose SQL Server installation components

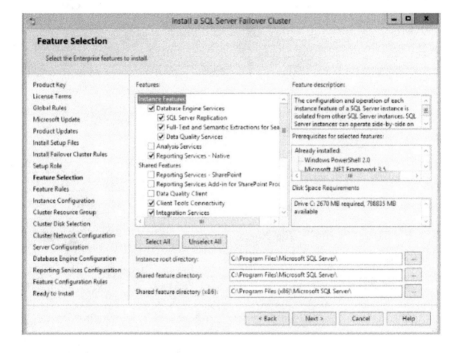

(3) Enter SQL Server cluster name. Example here: SQL_Cluster

(4) Check available storage can be used by SQL Server database on the cluster.

Microsoft SQL Server cluster will automatically choose the smallest disk storage as Quorum Disk. Quorum Disk is reserved as clustering quorum purpose. No SQL data can be installed on that disk.

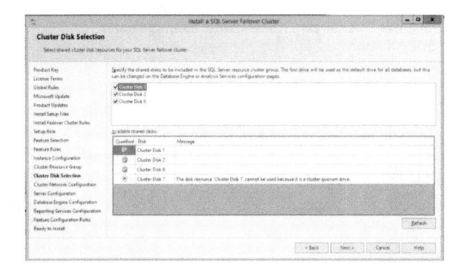

(5) Enter SQL Server cluster IP address and network Subnet
Mask

(6) Enter SQL Server service account name and password.

They are Active Directory accounts to handle SQL Server services.

(7) Enter SQL Server database directory and Temp DB directory

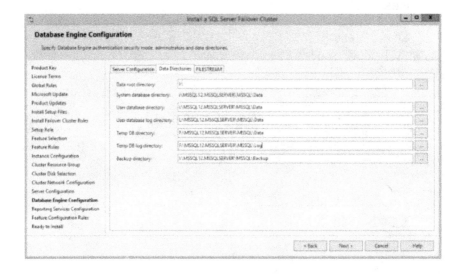

(8) Start SQL Server installation

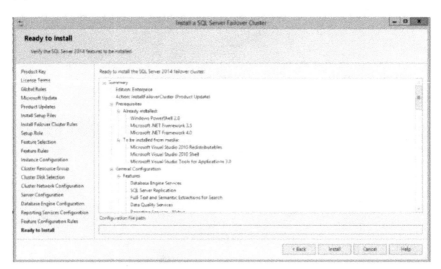

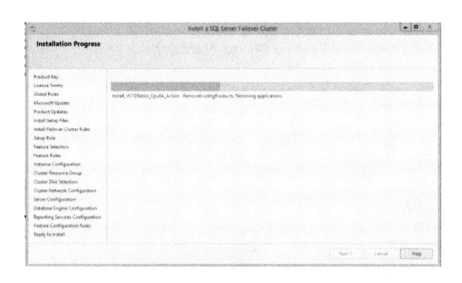

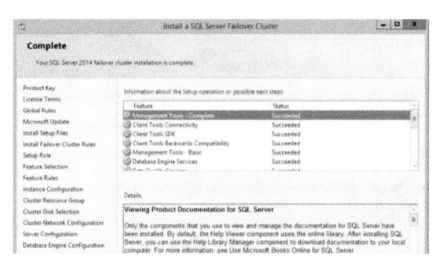

(9) After the installation is completed, check SQL cluster server status from Failover Cluster Manager.

Inside Other Resources both SQL Server and SQL Server Agent should be online.

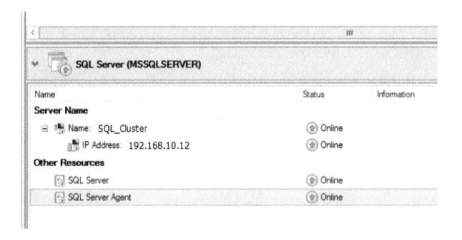

Part 2 installation is completed.

After Part 2 installation is completed, continue to Part 3 installation on the secondary node (**WIN_Server2**).

3. SQL SERVER CLUSTER (PART 3)

This part describes the installation of SQL Server cluster on node 2 server, WIN_Server2.

(1) Start the new SQL Server installation from node 2

Choose Add Node to a SQL Server Failover Cluster in installation menu.

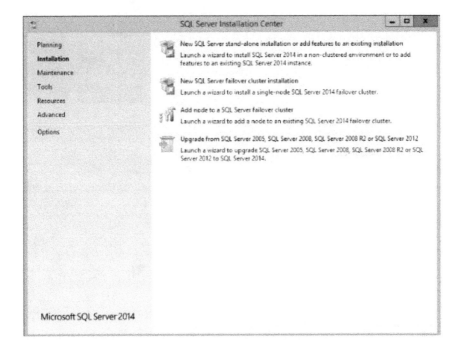

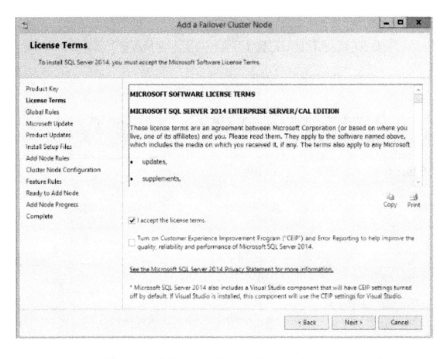

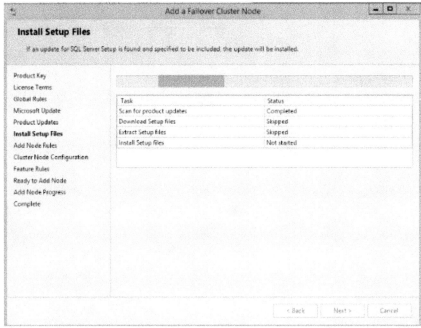

(2) Choose SQL_Cluster as Cluster Network Name

(3) Enter IP address of the secondary node and Subnet information

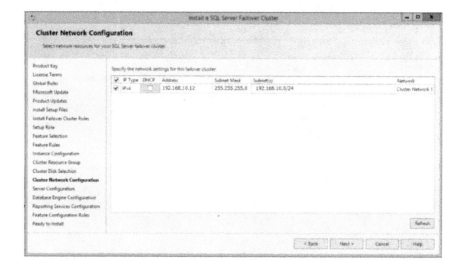

4) Enter SQL Server service account name and password. They are Active Directory accounts to handle SQL Server services.

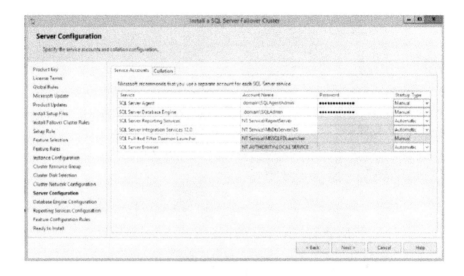

(5) Start to install SQL Server

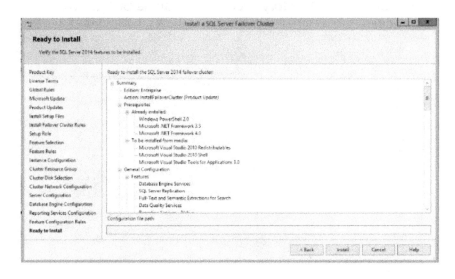

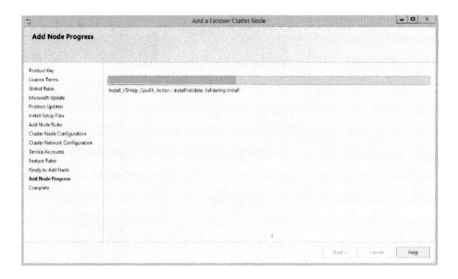

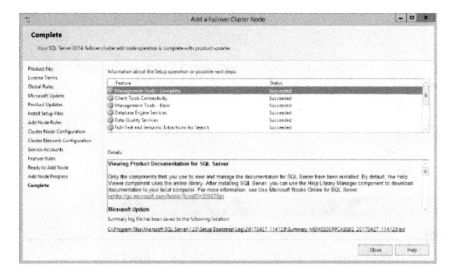

(6) After the installation is completed, from Failover Cluster Manage check the online status of SQL Server Cluster instance

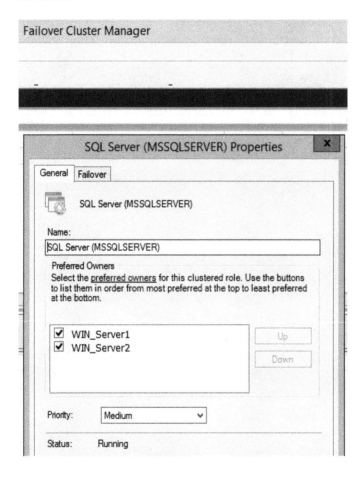

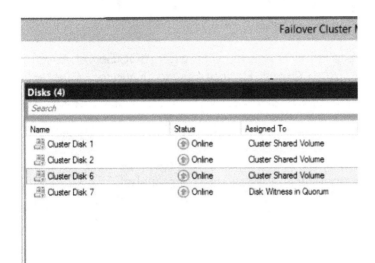

Disks (4)		
Search		
Name	Status	Assigned To
Cluster Disk 1	Online	Cluster Shared Volume
Cluster Disk 2	Online	Cluster Shared Volume
Cluster Disk 6	Online	Cluster Shared Volume
Cluster Disk 7	Online	Disk Witness in Quorum

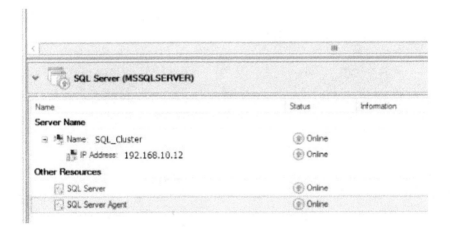

SQL Server (MSSQLSERVER)

Name	Status	Information
Server Name		
Name: SQL_Cluster	Online	
IP Address: 192.168.10.12	Online	
Other Resources		
SQL Server	Online	
SQL Server Agent	Online	

Once new SQL cluster online status are verified, **Part 3** installation is completed.

4. SQL SERVER CLUSTER (PART 4)

This part installation is needed only when SQL Server Agent is missing from **Other Resources** in **Failover Cluster Manager**.

Missing SQL Server Agent in Other Resources will cause Failover Cluster Manager running incorrectly.

The example shows as the following screenshot:

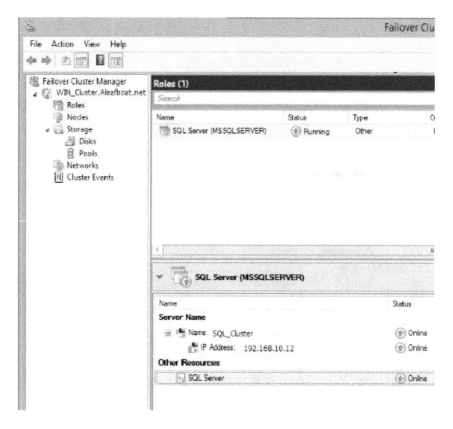

The following steps list how to add SQL Server Agent into **Other Resources** in Failover Cluster Manager.

(1) From Windows PowerShell run the following commands:

Import-Module FailoverClusters

Add-ClusterResourceType "SQL Server Agent"
C:\Windows\System32\SQAGTRES.DLL

(2) From Failover Cluster Manager, choose Add Resource menu, then choose SQL Server Agent

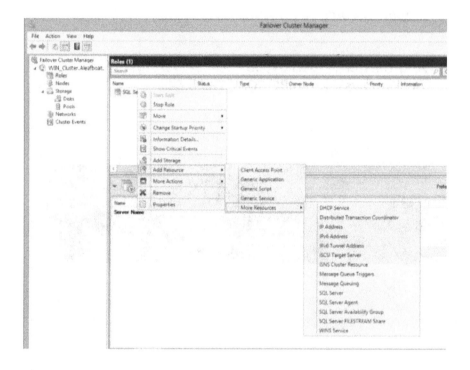

(3) Right click newly added SQL Server agent, and choose
Properties. Add SQL_Cluster as VirtualServerName.

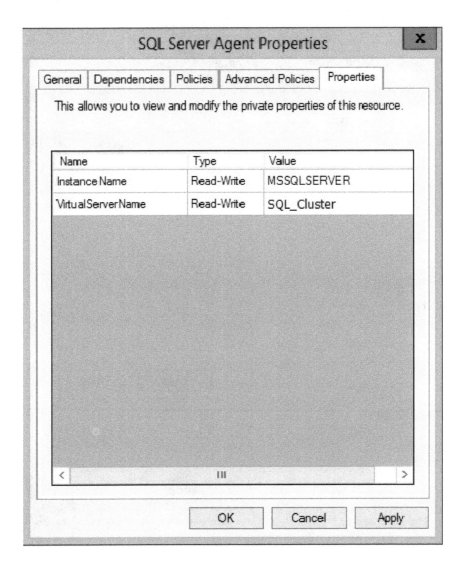

(4) In Dependencies tab choose SQL Server

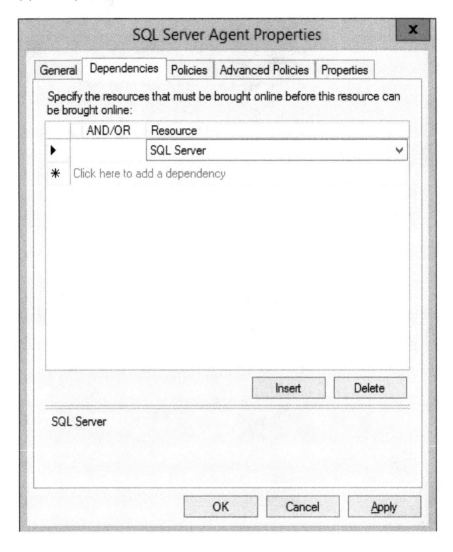

(5) In Advanced Policies tab check available node 1 server: WIN_Server1.

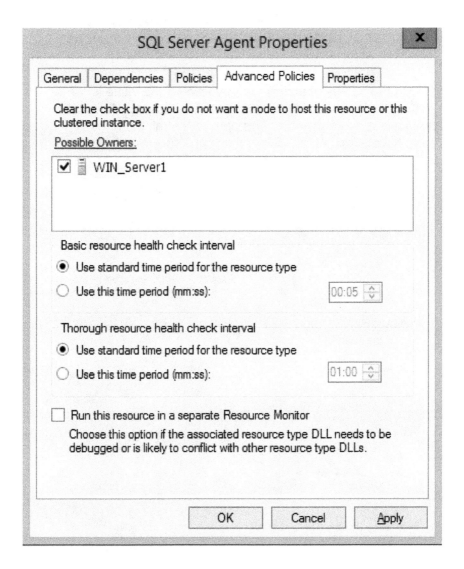

(6) Open Windows Registry and then go to

HKEY_LOCAL_MACHINE\SOFTWARE\Microsoft SQL Server\MSSQL10_50.INSTANCENAME\ConfigurationState

Check the values of all the registry kays. If the value is great than 1, it means that there was a failure occurred during the installation. Note the following picture that all the registry keys have a value of 2.

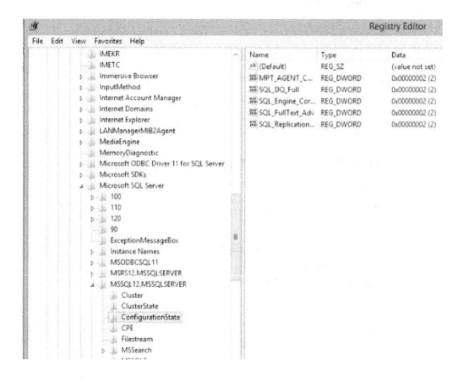

(7) Change registry key value to 1 for each item.

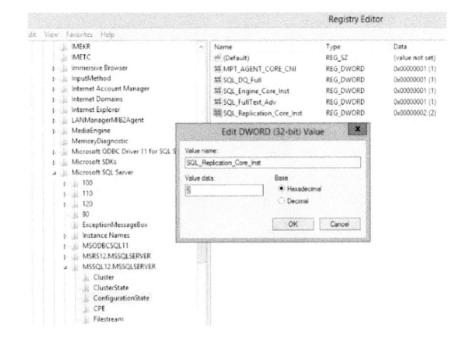

(8) After all above steps completed, check Other Resources in the Failover Cluster Manager to find both SQL Server and SQL Server Agent.

If both SQL Server and SQL Server Agent located under Other Resources, **Part 4** installation is completed.

Change Collation on SQL Server 2014

Collation refers to a set of rules that determine how data is sorted and compared.

Character data is sorted according to the rules that define the correct character sequence.

SQL Server collation is obtained during the installation. However SQL Server collation can be changed after installation. The following discussion provides the steps to change SQL Server collation.

(1) Find current SQL Server collation from SQL Server Management Studio

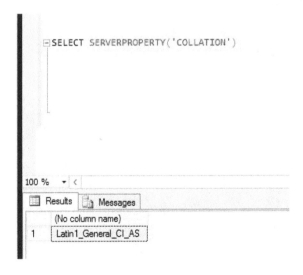

It shows the current collation: **Latin1_General_CI_AS**

Collation can also be found from SQL Server property:

Product	Microsoft SQL Server Enterprise (64-bit)
Operating System	Microsoft Windows NT 6.3 (9600)
Platform	NT x64
Version	12.0.5207.0
Language	English (United States)
Memory	32638 MB
Processors	24
Root Directory	C:\Program Files\Microsoft SQL Server\MSSQL12
Server Collation	Latin1_General_CI_AS
Is Clustered	False
Is HADR Enabled	False
Is XTP Supported	True

Name
Name of the server and instance.

(2) Stop SQL Server service

SMB Witness	SMB Witnes...	Manual (Trigger Start)
SNMP Trap	Receives tra...	Manual
Software Protection	Enables the ...	Automatic (Delayed Start, Trigger St...
Special Administration Console Helper	Allows adm...	Disabled
Spot Verifier	Verifies pot...	Manual (Trigger Start)
SQL Full-text Filter Daemon Launcher (MSS...	Service to la...	Manual
SQL Server (Aleafboat_SQL1)	Provides sto...	Automatic
SQL Server Agent (Aleafboat_SQL1)	Executes jo...	Automatic
SQL Server Browser	Provides SQ... Running	Automatic
SQL Server Integration Services 12.0	Provides m...	Automatic
SQL Server Reporting Services	Manages, e...	Automatic
SQL Server VSS Writer	Provides th... Running	Automatic
SSDP Discovery	Discovers n...	Disabled
Storage Tiers Management	Optimizes t...	Manual
Superfetch	Maintains a...	Disabled

(3) Open command prompt to the following path:

C:\Program Files\Microsoft SQL Server\MSSQL12.MSSQLSERVER\MSSQL\Binn

```
C:\>cd C:\Program Files\Microsoft SQL Server\MSSQL12.MSSQLSERVER\MSSQL\Binn

C:\Program Files\Microsoft SQL Server\MSSQL12.MSSQLSERVER\MSSQL\Binn>dir sqlservr.exe
Volume in drive C has no label.
Volume Serial Number is 9C5C-4EA1

Directory of C:\Program Files\Microsoft SQL Server\MSSQL12.MSSQLSERVER\MSSQL\Binn

08/19/2016  08:10 PM        372,416 sqlservr.exe
               1 File(s)        372,416 bytes
               0 Dir(s)  77,772,222,464 bytes free

C:\Program Files\Microsoft SQL Server\MSSQL12.MSSQLSERVER\MSSQL\Binn>_
```

(4) Run the following command from Command Prompt:

sqlservr -m -T4022 -T3659 -s"SQL_INSTANCE"
-q"SQL_Latin1_General_CP1_CI_AS"

```
\MSSQL\Binn
Binn>sqlservr -m -T4022 -T3659 -s"Aleafboat_SQL1" -q"SQL_Latin1_General_CP1_CI_AS"_
```

In above command example:

- -m: SQL Server single user mode
- -T: trace flag turned on at startup
- -s: sql server instance name: Aleafboat_SQL1
- -q: new collation: SQL_Latin1_General_CP1_CI_AS

Wait for command process completed.

```
14:46:51.54 spid9s    index restored for ReportServer.ChunkData.
14:46:51.54 spid9s    index restored for ReportServer.Schedule.
14:46:51.54 spid9s    index restored for ReportServer.RunningJobs.
14:46:51.54 spid9s    index restored for ReportServer.ServerParametersInstance.
14:46:51.71 spid9s    index restored for ReportServerTempDB.syspriorities.
14:46:51.71 spid9s    index restored for ReportServerTempDB.sysprufiles.
14:46:51.72 spid9s    index restored for ReportServerTempDB.sysowners.
14:46:51.72 spid9s    index restored for ReportServerTempDB.sysdbreg.
14:46:51.73 spid9s    index restored for ReportServerTempDB.sysschobjs.
14:46:51.73 spid9s    index restored for ReportServerTempDB.syscolpars.
14:46:51.73 spid9s    index restored for ReportServerTempDB.sysxlgns.
14:46:51.74 spid9s    index restored for ReportServerTempDB.sysxsrvs.
14:46:51.74 spid9s    index restored for ReportServerTempDB.sysnsobjs.
14:46:51.74 spid9s    index restored for ReportServerTempDB.syscerts.
14:46:51.74 spid9s    index restored for ReportServerTempDB.sysrmtlgns.
14:46:51.74 spid9s    index restored for ReportServerTempDB.sysxprops.
14:46:51.74 spid9s    index restored for ReportServerTempDB.sysscalartypes.
14:46:51.74 spid9s    index restored for ReportServerTempDB.sysidxstats.
14:46:51.74 spid9s    index restored for ReportServerTempDB.sysendpts.
14:46:51.74 spid9s    index restored for ReportServerTempDB.sysclsobjs.
14:46:51.74 spid9s    index restored for ReportServerTempDB.sysremsvcbinds.
14:46:51.74 spid9s    index restored for ReportServerTempDB.sysrts.
14:46:51.74 spid9s    index restored for ReportServerTempDB.sysasymkeys.
14:46:51.74 spid9s    index restored for ReportServerTempDB.syssqlguids.
14:46:51.74 spid9s    index restored for ReportServerTempDB.syssoftobjrefs.
14:46:51.77 spid9s    index restored for ReportServerTempDB.SessionLock.
14:46:51.78 spid9s    index restored for ReportServerTempDB.SessionData.
14:46:51.78 spid9s    index restored for ReportServerTempDB.SnapshotData.
14:46:51.78 spid9s    index restored for ReportServerTempDB.ChunkData.
14:46:51.78 spid9s    index restored for ReportServerTempDB.PersistedStream.
14:46:51.78 spid9s    index restored for ReportServerTempDB.SegmentedChunk.
14:46:51.78 spid9s    index restored for ReportServerTempDB.DBUpgradeHistory.
14:46:51.79 spid9s    index restored for ReportServerTempDB.TempCatalog.
14:46:51.79 spid9s    index restored for ReportServerTempDB.TempDataSets.
14:46:51.79 spid9s    The default collation was successfully changed.
14:46:51.79 spid9s    Recovery is complete. This is an informational message only. No user action is required.
```

(5) Start SQL Server service

SNMP Trap	Receives tra...		Manual
Software Protection	Enables the ...	Running	Automatic (Delayed Start, Trigger Start)
Special Administration Console Helper	Allows adm...		Disabled
Spot Verifier	Verifies pot...		Manual (Trigger Start)
SQL Server (Aleafboat_SQL1)	Provides sto...	Running	Automatic
SQL Server Agent (Aleafboat_SQL1)	Executes jo...	Running	Automatic
SQL Server Browser	Provides SQ...	Running	Automatic
SQL Server Integration Services 12.0	Provides m...		Automatic
SQL Server Reporting Services	Manages, e...		Automatic
SQL Server VSS Writer	Provides th...	Running	Automatic
SSDP Discovery	Discovers n...		Disabled
Storage Tiers Management	Optimizes t...		Manual

(6) Check new SQL Server collation by SQL Server
Management Studio

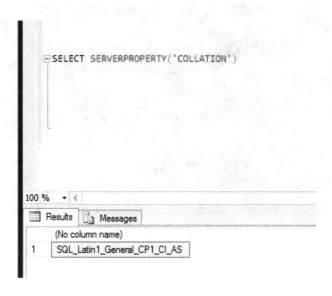

Collation can also be checked from server property:

Product	Microsoft SQL Server Enterprise (64-bit)
Operating System	Microsoft Windows NT 6.3 (9600)
Platform	NT x64
Version	12.0.5207.0
Language	English (United States)
Memory	32638 MB
Processors	24
Root Directory	C:\Program Files\Microsoft SQL Server\MSSQL12
Server Collation	SQL_Latin1_General_CP1_CI_AS
Is Clustered	False
Is HADR Enabled	False
Is XTP Supported	True

Name
Name of the server and instance.

Changing collation on SQL Server 2014 is completed.

ODBC Configuration (Part 1 – Oracle)

An ODBC driver uses Open Database Connectivity (ODBC) interface by Microsoft that allows applications to access data in database management systems (DBMS) using SQL as a standard for accessing the data.

The following steps list Windows ODBC configuration to connect to Oracle database. This ODBC connection can be used by Microsoft SQL Server to access Oracle database.

(1) Download Oracle client software from Oracle official web site

Database > Database 11g > Downloads

Overview	**Downloads**	Documentation	Learn More	Community

Oracle Database 11*g* Release 2 (11.2.0.1.0)
Standard Edition, Standard Edition One, and Enterprise Edition

You must accept the OTN License Agreement to download this software.
○ Accept License Agreement | ○ Decline License Agreement

Oracle Database 11*g* Release 2 (11.2.0.1.0) for Microsoft Windows (x64)
 ⬇ win64_11gR2_database_1of2.zip (1,213,501,989 bytes) (cksum - 3906682109)
 ⬇ win64_11gR2_database_2of2.zip (1,007,988,954 bytes) (cksum - 1232608515)

Directions
 1. All files are in the .zip format. There is an unzip utility here if you need one.
 2. Download and unzip both files to the same directory.
 3. Installation guides and general Oracle Database 11g documentation are here.
 4. Review the certification matrix for this product here.

Oracle Database 11*g* Release 2 Client (11.2.0.1.0) for Microsoft Windows (x64)
 ⬇ win64_11gR2_client.zip (615,698,264 bytes) (cksum - 2947608743)

Contains the Oracle Client Libraries. Download if you want the client libraries only.

Oracle Database 11*g* Release 2 Grid Infrastructure (11.2.0.1.0) for Microsoft Windows (x64)
 ⬇ win64_11gR2_grid.zip (715,166,425 bytes) (cksum - 3127109177)

 Contains the Grid Infrastructure Software including Oracle Clusterware, Automated

(2) Install Oracle Client software on Windows Server which SQL Server is located

Documents library
11gR2_client_64bit

Name	Size
client	
win64_11gR2_client	601,268 KB

Documents library
client

Name	Size
doc	
install	
response	
stage	
setup	334 KB
setup	1 KB
welcome	5 KB

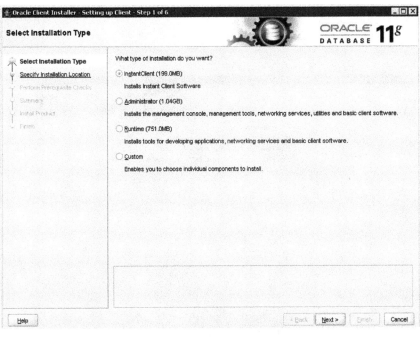

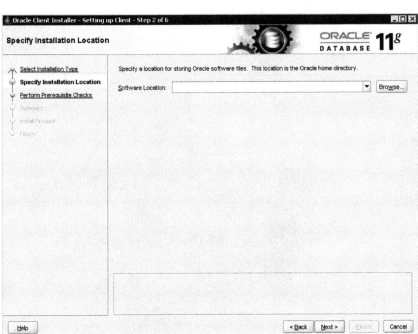

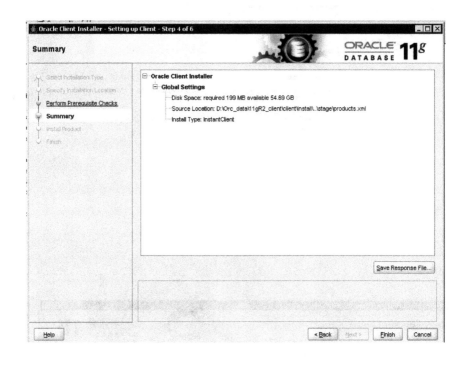

(3) Check TNSNAMES file created on the server in the following path:

\product\11.2.0\client_1\network\admin\TNSNAMES.ORA
Verify SID and Oracle server IP address in the file:

```
PROD =
     (DESCRIPTION =
        (ADDRESS_LIST =
          (ADDRESS =
              (COMMUNITY = tcp.world)
              (PROTOCOL = TCP)
              (Host = 192.168.20.28)
              (Port = 1521)
           )
         )
         (CONNECT_DATA = (SID = PROD)
         )
     )
```

(4) On Windows Server open "ODBC Data Source Administrator"

From System DSN tab click Add button:

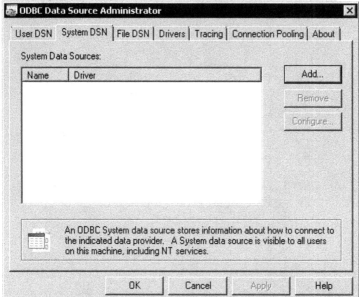

(5) From Drivers tab choose Oracle Drive "Oracle in OraClient11g", then click OK button:

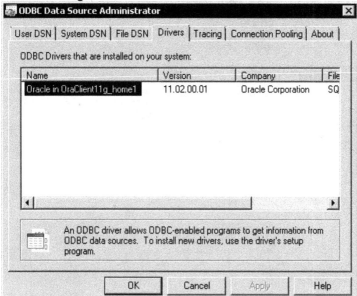

(6) Enter Oracle server information in Oracle ODBC Driver Configuration:

Oracle ODBC Driver Configuration

Data Source Name	ORA_SRV1
Description	
TNS Service Name	PROD
User ID	ORA_USER

OK
Cancel
Help
Test Connection

Application | Oracle | Workarounds | SQLServer Migration |

Enable Result Sets ☑   Enable Query Timeout ☑   Read-Only Connection ☐

Enable Closing Cursors ☐   Enable Thread Safety ☑

Batch Autocommit Mode   [Commit only if all statements succeed ▼]

Numeric Settings   [Use Oracle NLS settings ▼]

Oracle ODBC Driver Configuration

Data Source Name	ORA_SRV1
Description	
TNS Service Name	PROD
User ID	ORA_USER

OK
Cancel
Help
Test Connection

Application | Oracle | Workarounds | SQLServer Migration |

Fetch Buffer Size [64000]

Enable LOBs ☑

Enable Statement Caching ☐

Cache Buffer Size [20]

Failover
Enable Failover ☑
Retry [10]
Delay [10]

51

Oracle ODBC Driver Configuration

Data Source Name: ORA_SRV1

Description:

TNS Service Name: PROD

User ID: ORA_USER

OK
Cancel
Help
Test Connection

Application | Oracle | **Workarounds** | SQLServer Migration |

Bind TIMESTAMP as DATE	☐	Disable SQLDescribeParam	☐
Force SQL_WCHAR Support	☐	Bind NUMBER As FLOAT	☐
Disable Microsoft Transaction Server	☑	Disable RULE Hint	☑
Set Metadata Id Default to SQL_TRUE	☐		

Oracle ODBC Driver Configuration

Data Source Name: ORA_SRV1

Description:

TNS Service Name: PROD

User ID: ORA_USER

OK
Cancel
Help
Test Connection

Application | Oracle | Workarounds | **SQLServer Migration** |

Enable EXEC Syntax ☐   Schema [▼]

(7) Perform Oracle server connection test:

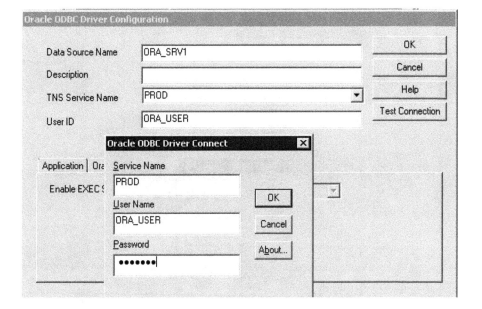

(8) Review test result

If ODBC connection test is successful, this ODBC can be used to connect SQL Server to Oracle database server.

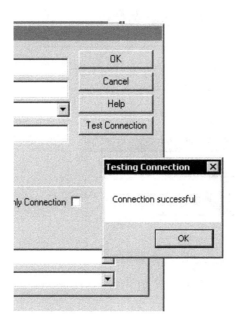

It is completed for **Part 1: Windows ODBC Configuration for Oracle Database.**

ODBC configuration **Part 2** will cover Microsoft ODBC configuration for **Informix server.**

ODBC Configuration (Part 2 – Informix)

An ODBC driver uses Open Database Connectivity (ODBC) interface by Microsoft that allows applications to access data in database management systems (DBMS) using SQL as a standard for accessing the data.

Windows ODBC Configuration for Informix Database

The following discussion lists the steps of ODBC configuration to connect to IBM Informix Server.

This ODBC connection can be used by Microsoft SQL Server Integration Services (SSIS) to access Informix database.

(1) Install Informix Client 4.1 software on Windows Server which SQL Server is located

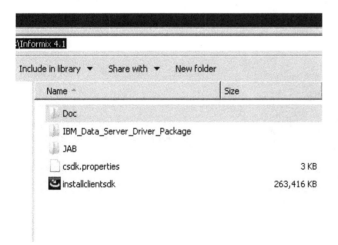

(2) The installation is started by running program:
installclientsdk

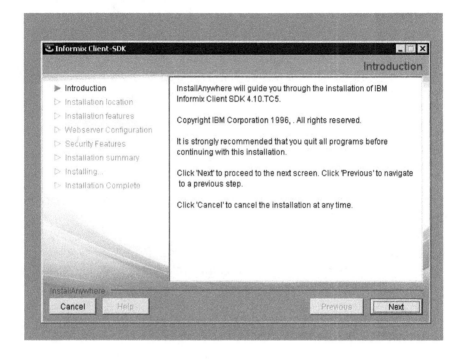

(3) Click Next to continue:

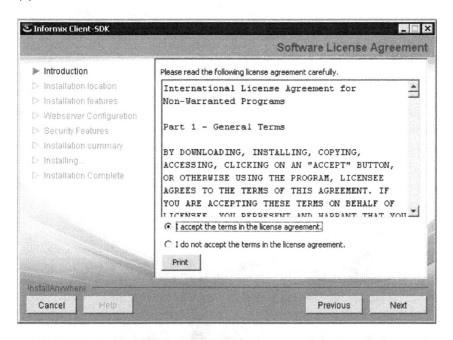

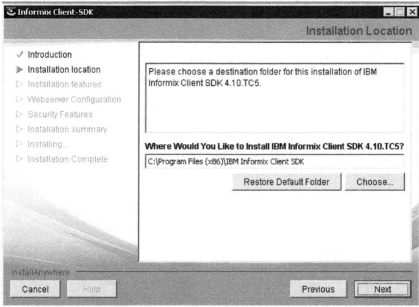

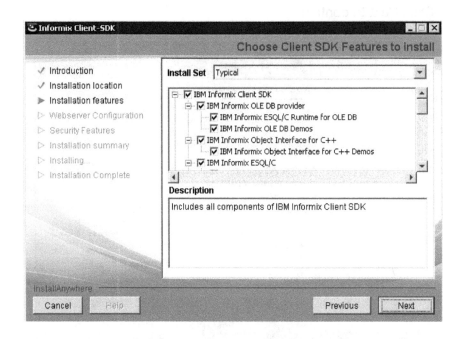

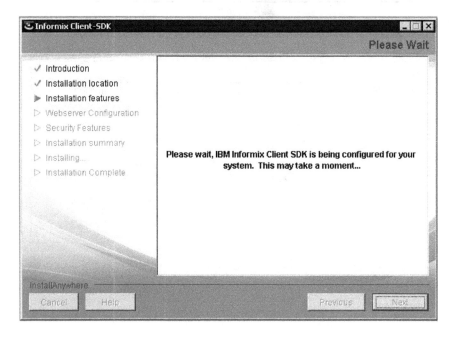

58

(4) After software installation completed, open Windows Server open "**ODBC Data Source Administrator**"

From System DSN tab click Add button:

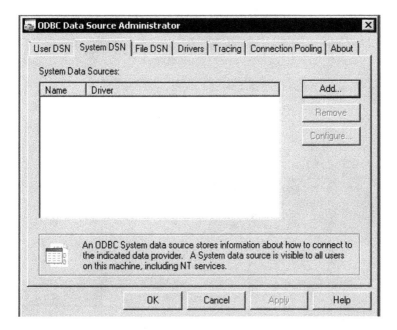

(5) In Create New Data Source menu choose "IBM INFORMIX ODBC DRIVER", then click Finish button.

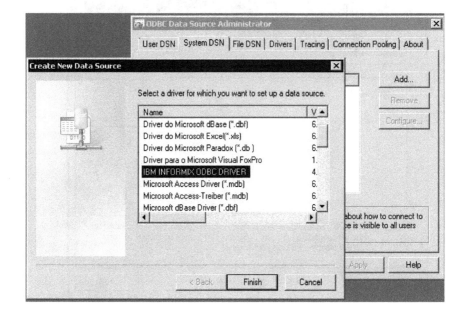

6) From ODBC Data Source Administrator to start ODBC
Driver Setup. In General tab enter Data Source Name:

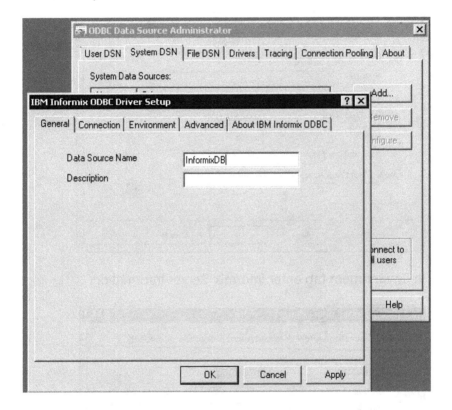

In Connection tab enter Informix server connection information:

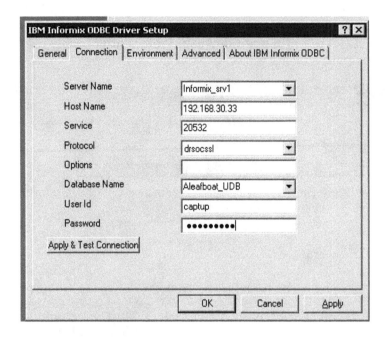

In Environment tab enter Informix Server information:

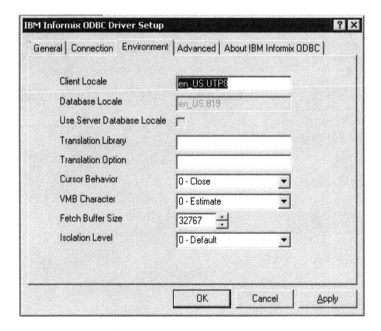

In Advanced tab check Auto Commit Optimization option:

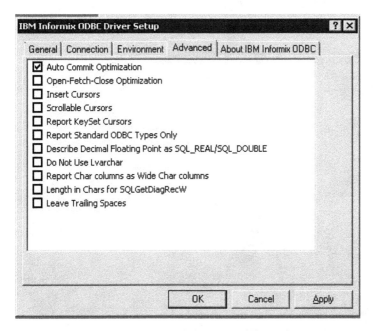

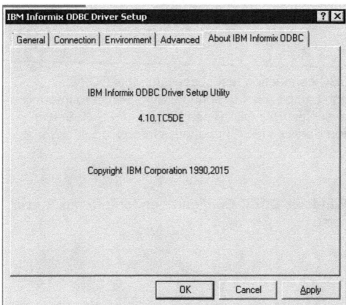

(7) Perform ODBC connection test to Informix server by click Apply & Test Connection button:

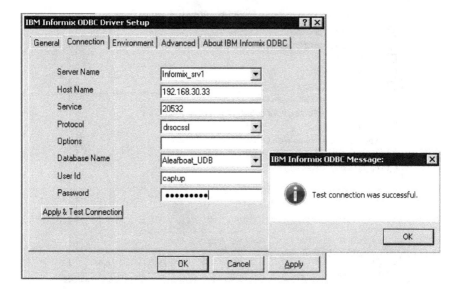

(8) If ODBC connection test successful, this ODBC connection can be used to connect SQL Server to Informix database server. This ODBC can be used for SQL Server Integration Services (SSIS) to access Informix database.

Part 2: **Windows ODBC Configuration for Informix Server** is completed.

ODBC Configuration Part 3
SQL Server

The following discussion lists the steps of Windows ODBC configuration to SQL Server. This ODBC connection can be used by Microsoft SQL Server Integration Services (SSIS) to input and export data.

(1) On Windows Server start ODBC Data Source Administrator. In System DSN tab click Add button.

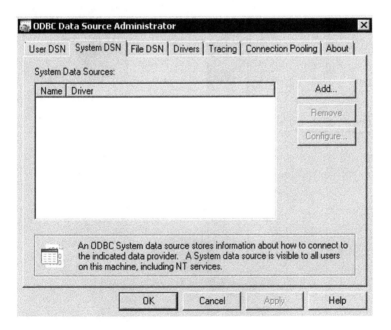

(2) From Create New Data Source window, choose SQL Server drive from list:

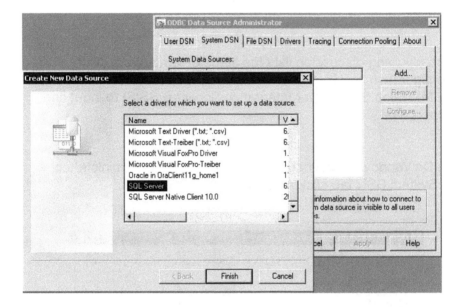

(3) Enter new ODBC connection name and SQL Server name.
Click Next.

Example here new ODBC connection name is DS01.

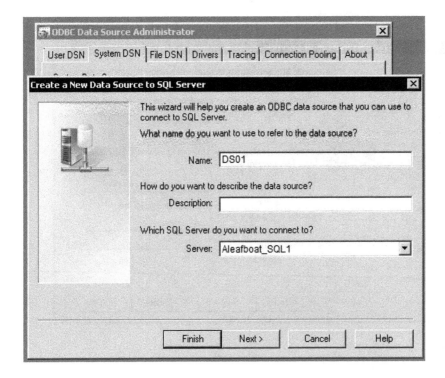

(4) Choose Windows authentication or SQL Server authentication. Click Client Configuration button:

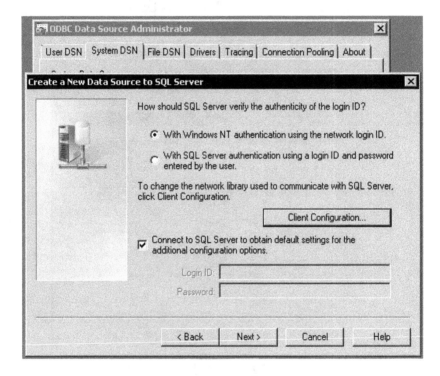

(5) Review SQL Server Connection parameters. Click OK.

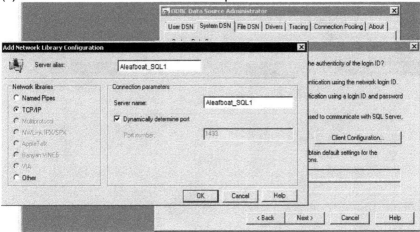

(6) In new popup window click Next button. Then click Finish button:

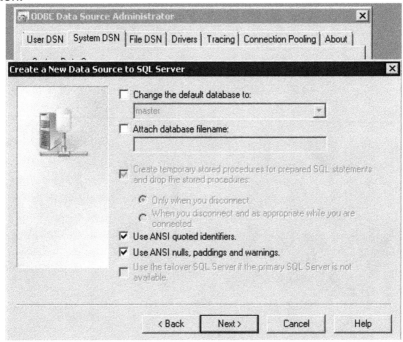

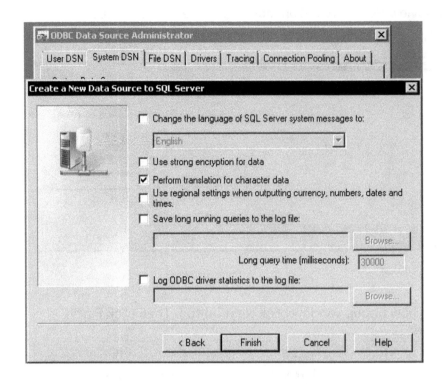

(7) Click Test Data Source button to test connection:

(8) If test is successful, click OK button to save the new
ODBC configuration. Example name here is DS01.

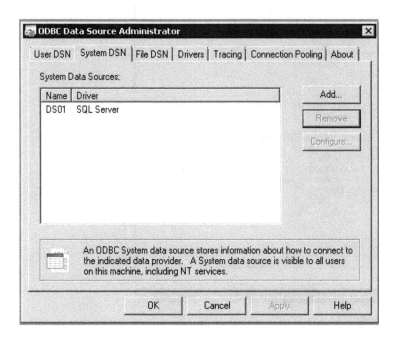

ODBC connection can be configured for local SQL Server or
remote SQL server. It can be used to handle import and
export data tasks, such as by Microsoft SQL Server
Integration Services (SSIS).

Part 3 ODBC Configuration for SQL Server is completed.

Scripts to Monitor SQL Server
Part 1

It is convenient to use SQL scripts to monitor SQL server activities, such as services, memory and disk activities.

The following SQL scripts are used for monitoring SQL Server activities.

Part 1: Monitor SQL Server Services
Part 2: Monitor SQL Server memory usage
Part 3: Monitor SQL Server disk activities

Part 1:
SQL script to monitor SQL Server Services activity

Running the following T-SQL scripts from SQL Server Management Studio on SQL Server 2014 to monitor the current activities of SQL Server Service and SQL Agent Service.

```
SET NOCOUNT ON;

SELECT
@@servername as [Server Name], servicename as
[Service Name], process_id,
startup_type_desc as [startup type desc], status_desc as
[status desc],
last_startup_time as [last startup time], service_account
as [service account],
is_clustered, cluster_nodename as [ cluster nodename],
CASE
WHEN
[filename] like '%sqlservr.exe%' THEN 'SQLSERVR.EXE'
WHEN
[filename] like '%SQLAGENT.EXE%' THEN
'SQLAGENT.EXE'
ELSE '' END as [filename],
CONVERT(VARCHAR(20),GETDATE(),120) as [Date Time]
FROM
sys.dm_server_services WITH (NOLOCK);
```

Example output as the following:

Server Name	Service Name	process_id	startup_type	status desc	last_startup_time
SQL1	SQL Server (MSSQLSERVER)	3125	Automatic	Running	4/5/2018
SQL1	SQL Server (MSSQLSERVER)	6504	Automatic	Running	4/5/2018

service_account	is_clusteres	cluster_nodename	filename	Date Time
sql_service	N	NULL	SQLSERVER.EXE	4/5/2018 2:23
sql_service	N	NULL	SQLAGENT.EXE	4/5/2018 2:23

Scripts to Monitor SQL Server
Part 2

It is convenient to use SQL scripts to monitor SQL server activities, such as services, memory and disk activity.

The following SQL scripts are used for monitoring SQL Server activities.

Part 1: Monitor SQL Server Services
Part 2: Monitor SQL Server memory usage
Part 3: Monitor SQL Server disk activities

Part 2:
Monitor SQL Server memory usage

Run the following T-SQL codes on SQL Server 2014 to monitor SQL Server memory status:

```sql
SET NOCOUNT ON;

SELECT
@@SERVERNAME AS [Server Name],
total_physical_memory_kb/1024/1024 AS [Physical
Memory(GB)],
available_physical_memory_kb/1024/1024 AS [Available
Memory(GB)],
total_page_file_kb/1024/1024 AS [PageFile (GB)],
available_page_file_kb/1024/1024 AS [Available
PageFile(GB)],
system_cache_kb/1024/1024 AS [System Cache(GB)],
 CASE
 WHEN
system_memory_state_desc='Available physical memory
is high' then 'Available memory is high'
else 'memory is low'
END  AS [Memory State],
CONVERT(VARCHAR(20),GETDATE(),120) as [DateTime]
FROM
sys.dm_os_sys_memory WITH (NOLOCK);
```

Example output listed as the following:

Server Name	Physical Memory(GB)	Available Memory(GB)	Page File(GB)	Available PageFile(GB)	System Cache(GB)	Memory State	Date Time
SQL1	127	109	255	236	2	Available memory is high	12/5/2017 13:44

Scripts to Monitor SQL Server
Part 3

It is convenient to use SQL scripts to monitor SQL server activities, such as services, memory and disk activity.

The following SQL scripts are used for monitoring SQL Server activities.

Part 1: Monitor SQL Server Services
Part 2: Monitor SQL Server memory usage
Part 3: Monitor SQL Server disk activities

Part 3:
Monitor SQL Server disk activities

Run the following T-SQL scripts to monitor server disks activities on SQL Server 2014:

```
SET NOCOUNT ON;

SELECT
@@SERVERNAME as [Server Name], [Drive],
CASE
WHEN num_of_reads = 0 THEN 0
ELSE (io_stall_read_ms/num_of_reads)
END AS [Read Latency],
CASE
WHEN io_stall_write_ms = 0 THEN 0
ELSE (io_stall_write_ms/num_of_writes)
END AS [Write Latency],
CASE
WHEN (num_of_reads = 0 AND num_of_writes = 0)
THEN 0
ELSE (io_stall/(num_of_reads + num_of_writes))
END AS [Overall Latency],
CASE
WHEN num_of_reads = 0 THEN 0
ELSE (num_of_bytes_read/num_of_reads)
END AS [Avg Bytes/Read],
CASE
WHEN io_stall_write_ms = 0 THEN 0
ELSE (num_of_bytes_written/num_of_writes)
END AS [Avg Bytes/Write],
CASE
WHEN (num_of_reads = 0 AND num_of_writes = 0)
THEN 0
ELSE ((num_of_bytes_read +
num_of_bytes_written)/(num_of_reads +
num_of_writes))
END AS [Avg Bytes/Transfer],
CONVERT(VARCHAR(20),GETDATE(),120) as [Date
Time]
```

```
FROM
 (SELECT LEFT(UPPER(mf.physical_name), 2) AS Drive,
SUM(num_of_reads) AS num_of_reads,
SUM(io_stall_read_ms) AS io_stall_read_ms,
SUM(num_of_writes) AS num_of_writes,
SUM(io_stall_write_ms) AS io_stall_write_ms,
SUM(num_of_bytes_read) AS num_of_bytes_read,
SUM(num_of_bytes_written) AS num_of_bytes_written,
SUM(io_stall) AS io_stall
FROM
sys.dm_io_virtual_file_stats(NULL, NULL) AS vfs
INNER JOIN sys.master_files AS mf –WITH (NOLOCK)
ON vfs.database_id = mf.database_id AND vfs.file_id =
mf.file_id
GROUP BY LEFT(UPPER(mf.physical_name), 2)) AS tab
ORDER BY [Overall Latency] OPTION (RECOMPILE);
```

Example output as the following:

Server Name	Drive	Read Latency	Write Latency	Overall Latency	Avg Bytes/Read	Avg Bytes/Write	Avg Bytes/Transfer	Date Time
SQL1	E:	1	0	0	37247	7955	20336	12/5/2017 13:48
SQL1	H:	5	1	1	25498	13237	13591	12/5/2017 13:48
SQL1	T:	130	0	52	62647	9521	30759	12/5/2017 13:48

Index Defragmentation

Each time when insert, update, or delete operations occur in table, SQL Server Database Engine automatically modifies indexes in the table. Over time these modifications can cause the index information to become fragmented.

Heavily **fragmented indexes** can degrade query performance and cause the application to respond slowly, especially scan operations.

You can remedy index fragmentation by "reorganize" or "rebuild" an index.

These two methods on Microsoft SQL Server can reorganize or rebuild a fragmented index in by using SQL Server Management Studio or Transact-SQL.

Rebuilding an index drops and re-creates the index. This removes fragmentation, reclaims disk space by compacting the pages based on the specified or existing fill factor setting, and reorders the index rows in contiguous pages. Rebuilding an index can be executed online or offline.

Reorganizing an index uses minimal system resources. It defragments the leaf level of clustered and nonclustered indexes on tables and views by physically reordering the leaf-level pages to match the logical, left to right, order of the leaf nodes. Reorganizing also compacts the index pages. Reorganizing an index is always executed online.
Using the following steps to review and remedy index fragmentation on SQL Server.

Steps to Rebuild Fragmented Index

(1) Search indexes with average fragmentation over 80 percent in SQL_USD1 database

From SQL Server Management Studio run this SQL query:

USE SQL_USD1;
GO
SELECT a.object_id, a.index_id, b.name as index_name,
avg_fragmentation_in_percent
FROM sys.dm_db_index_physical_stats (DB_ID(), NULL,
NULL, NULL, NULL) AS a
JOIN sys.indexes AS b
ON a.object_id = b.object_id AND a.index_id = b.index_id
WHERE avg_fragmentation_in_percent > 80.0 AND
a.index_id > 0

Fragmented indexes listed here:

```
-----------------------------------------------------------------------
object_id  | index_id |    index_name      | avg_fragmentation_in_percent
-----------------------------------------------------------------------
251143940  |    5     | idx_udb_rep1       |   83.2116788321168
635144608  |    7     | idx_test_view      |   81.6176470588235
326262751  |    2     | idx_test_pertn     |   95.6521739130435
296315403  |    1     | idx_coll_serv_daily |  83.4760383386581
-----------------------------------------------------------------------
```

(2) Collect the index information into a temporary table

Run the following SQL query from SQL Server Management Studio:

SELECT a.object_id, a.index_id, b.name as index_name,
avg_fragmentation_in_percent
INTO #frag_index
FROM sys.dm_db_index_physical_stats (DB_ID(), NULL,
NULL, NULL, NULL) AS a
JOIN sys.indexes AS b
ON a.object_id = b.object_id AND a.index_id = b.index_id
WHERE avg_fragmentation_in_percent > 80.0 AND
a.index_id > 0

(3) Using following cursor to REBUILD fragmented indexes

```
SET NOCOUNT ON;
DECLARE @object_id int;
DECLARE @index_id int;
DECLARE @index_name nvarchar(100);
DECLARE @schema_name nvarchar(130);
DECLARE @object_name nvarchar(100);
DECLARE @command nvarchar(1000);
DECLARE tune_index CURSOR FOR
SELECT object_id, index_id, index_name FROM
#frag_index;

OPEN tune_index;
FETCH NEXT
    FROM tune_index
    INTO @object_id, @index_id, @index_name;

WHILE @@FETCH_STATUS = 0
BEGIN
SELECT  @object_name = o.name,  @schema_name =
s.name
    FROM sys.objects AS o
    JOIN sys.schemas as s ON s.schema_id =
o.schema_id
    WHERE o.object_id = @object_id;
```

```
SET @command = N'ALTER INDEX ' + @index_name
+ ' ON ' + @schema_name + '.' + @object_name + '
REBUILD';
    EXEC (@command);
    FETCH NEXT  FROM tune_index
    INTO @object_id, @index_id, @index_name
END;

CLOSE tune_index;
DEALLOCATE tune_index;
DROP TABLE #frag_index;
GO
```

After the indexes rebuild run SQL query in **step (1)** to review
the newly rebuild index fragmentation status.

Replacing **REBUILD** to **REORGANIZE** in the same cursor
can reorganize the indexes online.

PowerShell for SQL Server (Part 1)

Windows **PowerShell** is scripting language by using command-line interface.

The advantage of PowerShell is it provides Windows users with an opportunity to script these commands, enabling them to be automated, scheduled, and run multiple times.

Windows PowerShell integrates with the Microsoft .NET Framework. PowerShell uses SQL Server Management Objects (SMO) to connect to SQL Server. SMO can access the SQL Server related objects, features, and functionalities.

(1) Start Windows PowerShell from SQL Server Management Studio:

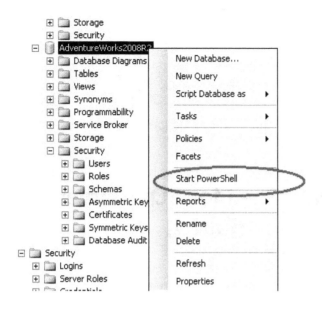

(2) Using SMO class library to connect SQL Server

The following PowerShell script uses SMO to connect to SQL server and collect database information on local server:

```
[System.Reflection.Assembly]::LoadWithPartialName(
'Microsoft.SqlServer.SMO') | Out-Null
$sqlser = New-Object
('Microsoft.SqlServer.Management.Smo.Server')
'localhost'
$sqlser.Databases
```

(3) Review output results

```
Name                  Status   Recovery Model CompatLvl Collation                    Owner
----                  ------   -------------- --------- ---------                    -----
AdventureWorks2008R2  Normal   Simple               100 SQL_Latin1_General_CP1_CI_AS NET\SQLadmin
master                Normal   Simple               100 SQL_Latin1_General_CP1_CI_AS sa
model                 Normal   Full                 100 SQL_Latin1_General_CP1_CI_AS sa
msdb                  Normal   Simple               100 SQL_Latin1_General_CP1_CI_AS sa
ReportServer          Normal   Full                 100 SQL_Latin1_General_CP1_CI_AS NET\SQLadmin
ReportServerTempDB    Normal   Simple               100 SQL_Latin1_General_CP1_CI_AS NET\SQLadmin
tempdb                Normal   Simple               100 SQL_Latin1_General_CP1_CI_AS sa
```

(4) Run the following command to display all methods of the SMO object:

$sqlser| Get-Member | Where-Object{$_.MemberType -eq 'Method'}

Review the output results:

```
Name                                  MemberType Definition
----                                  ---------- ----------
Alter                                 Method     System.Void Alter(), System.Void Alter(bool overrideValueChecking)
AttachDatabase                        Method     System.Void AttachDatabase(string name, System.Collections.Specialized...
CompareUrn                            Method     int CompareUrn(Microsoft.SqlServer.Management.Sdk.Sfc.Urn urn1, Micros...
DeleteBackupHistory                   Method     System.Void DeleteBackupHistory(System.DateTime oldestDate), System.Vo...
Deny                                  Method     System.Void Deny(Microsoft.SqlServer.Management.Smo.ServerPermissionSe...
DetachDatabase                        Method     System.Void DetachDatabase(string databaseName, bool updateStatistics)...
DetachedDatabaseInfo                  Method     System.Data.DataTable DetachedDatabaseInfo(string mdfName)
Discover                              Method     System.Collections.Generic.List[System.Object] Discover()
EnumActiveCurrentSessionTraceFlags    Method     System.Data.DataTable EnumActiveCurrentSessionTraceFlags()
EnumActiveGlobalTraceFlags            Method     System.Data.DataTable EnumActiveGlobalTraceFlags()
EnumAvailableMedia                    Method     System.Data.DataTable EnumAvailableMedia(), System.Data.DataTable Enum...
EnumCollations                        Method     System.Data.DataTable EnumCollations()
EnumDatabaseMirrorWitnessRoles        Method     System.Data.DataTable EnumDatabaseMirrorWitnessRoles(), System.Data.Da...
EnumDetachedDatabaseFiles             Method     System.Collections.Specialized.StringCollection EnumDetachedDatabaseFi...
EnumDetachedLogFiles                  Method     System.Collections.Specialized.StringCollection EnumDetachedLogFiles(s...
```

(5) Run the following PowerShell command to get SQL server configuration information:

$sqlser.Configuration.Properties | Select-Object DisplayName, Number, Minimum, Maximum

Review the output results:

DisplayName	Number	Minimum	Maximum
recovery interval (min)	101	0	32767
allow updates	102	0	1
user connections	103	0	32767
locks	106	5000	2147483647
open objects	107	0	2147483647
fill factor (%)	109	0	100
disallow results from trig...	114	0	1
nested triggers	115	0	1
server trigger recursion	116	0	1
remote access	117	0	1
default language	124	0	9999
cross db ownership chaining	400	0	1
max worker threads	503	128	32767

PowerShell for SQL Server (Part 2)

Windows PowerShell uses SQL Server Management Objects (SMO) to connect to SQL Server. SMO can access the SQL Server related objects, features, and functionalities.

The following PowerShell scripts perform tasks:

(1) Connect to a SQL Server instance by using SQL Server SMO.

(2) PowerShell uses "Microsoft.SqlServer.Management.Smo.Scripter" class to script database from AdventureWorks2008R2 database and display the results on screen.

[System.Reflection.Assembly]::LoadWithPartialName('Mi crosoft.SqlServer.SMO') | Out-Null
$PWScripter=New-Object ("Microsoft.SqlServer.Management.Smo.Scripter")
$sqlser = New-Object ('Microsoft.SqlServer.Management.Smo.Server')
"localhost"
$PWScripter.Server=$sqlser
$PWScripter.Script($sqlser.databases["AdventureWorks2 008R2"])

Review the following output results:

```
CREATE DATABASE [AdventureWorks2008R2] ON  PRIMARY
( NAME = N'AdventureWorks2008R2_Data', FILENAME = N'D:\SQLfiles\AdventureWorks2008R2_Data.mdf' , SIZE =
200640KB , MAXSIZE = UNLIMITED, FILEGROWTH = 16384KB )
 LOG ON
( NAME = N'AdventureWorks2008R2_Log', FILENAME = N'D:\SQLfiles\AdventureWorks2008R2_log.LDF' , SIZE =
504KB , MAXSIZE = UNLIMITED, FILEGROWTH = 10%)
 COLLATE SQL_Latin1_General_CP1_CI_AS
ALTER DATABASE [AdventureWorks2008R2] SET COMPATIBILITY_LEVEL = 100
IF (1 = FULLTEXTSERVICEPROPERTY('IsFullTextInstalled'))
begin
EXEC [AdventureWorks2008R2].[dbo].[sp_fulltext_database] @action = 'enable'
end
ALTER DATABASE [AdventureWorks2008R2] SET ANSI_NULL_DEFAULT OFF
ALTER DATABASE [AdventureWorks2008R2] SET ANSI_NULLS ON
ALTER DATABASE [AdventureWorks2008R2] SET ANSI_PADDING ON
ALTER DATABASE [AdventureWorks2008R2] SET ANSI_WARNINGS ON
ALTER DATABASE [AdventureWorks2008R2] SET ARITHABORT ON
ALTER DATABASE [AdventureWorks2008R2] SET AUTO_CLOSE OFF
ALTER DATABASE [AdventureWorks2008R2] SET AUTO_CREATE_STATISTICS ON
ALTER DATABASE [AdventureWorks2008R2] SET AUTO_SHRINK OFF
ALTER DATABASE [AdventureWorks2008R2] SET AUTO_UPDATE_STATISTICS ON
ALTER DATABASE [AdventureWorks2008R2] SET CURSOR_CLOSE_ON_COMMIT OFF
ALTER DATABASE [AdventureWorks2008R2] SET CURSOR_DEFAULT  GLOBAL
ALTER DATABASE [AdventureWorks2008R2] SET CONCAT_NULL_YIELDS_NULL ON
ALTER DATABASE [AdventureWorks2008R2] SET NUMERIC_ROUNDABORT OFF
ALTER DATABASE [AdventureWorks2008R2] SET QUOTED_IDENTIFIER ON
ALTER DATABASE [AdventureWorks2008R2] SET RECURSIVE_TRIGGERS OFF
```

PowerShell for SQL Server (Part 3)

PowerShell script in Part 3 collects tables object information from AdventureWorks2008R2 database.

The output results include table schema names and table names from the database.

Save the following Powershell script as: **list_tables.ps1** file.

```
Param (
[string] $SQLSERVER,
[string] $DATABASE
)
$SqlConnection = New-Object
System.Data.SqlClient.SqlConnection
$SqlConnection.ConnectionString =
"Server=$SQLSERVER;Database=$DATABASE;Integrated
Security=True"
$SqlCmd = New-Object
System.Data.SqlClient.SqlCommand
$SqlCmd.CommandText = "select TABLE_SCHEMA,
TABLE_NAME from INFORMATION_SCHEMA.TABLES
WHERE TABLE_TYPE='BASE TABLE' ORDER BY 1,2"
$SqlCmd.Connection = $SqlConnection
$SqlAdapter = New-Object
System.Data.SqlClient.SqlDataAdapter
$SqlAdapter.SelectCommand = $SqlCmd
```

```
$DataSet = New-Object System.Data.DataSet
$SqlAdapter.Fill($DataSet)
$SqlConnection.Close()
$DataSet.Tables[0]
```

Run the following command from PowerShell:
.\list_tables.ps1 "localhost"
"AdventureWorks2008R2"

Review the output results:

TABLE_SCHEMA	TABLE_NAME
dbo	AWBuildVersion
dbo	DatabaseLog
dbo	ErrorLog
HumanResources	Department
HumanResources	Employee
HumanResources	EmployeeDepartmentHistory
HumanResources	EmployeePayHistory
HumanResources	JobCandidate
HumanResources	Shift
Person	Address
Person	AddressType
Person	BusinessEntity
Person	BusinessEntityAddress
Person	BusinessEntityContact
Person	ContactType
Person	CountryRegion
Person	EmailAddress

PowerShell for SQL Server (Part 4)

Windows Management Instrumentation (**WMI**) is Microsoft's primary technology for managing Windows systems. WMI includes a large collection of classes that represent various system components, which enables Windows-based operating systems to be monitored and controlled, both locally and remotely.

The following examples use **WMI** classes in PowerShell to obtain SQL Server information.

(1) Run the following PowerShell command to check SQL Server status:

Get-WmiObject -class Win32_Service | Where-Object {$_.Name -eq 'MSSQLSERVER'}

Review the output results:

```
ExitCode   : 0
Name       : MSSQLSERVER
ProcessId  : 2640
StartMode  : Auto
State      : Running
Status     : OK
```

(2) Run the following PowerShell script to collect local server hard drive information

get-wmiobject -class win32_volume | ft -auto DriveLetter, Label,`
@{Label="DiskSize(GB)";Expression={"{0:N0}" -F ($_.Capacity/1GB)}},`
@{Label="FreeSpace(GB)";Expression={"{0:N0}" -F ($_.Freespace/1GB)}}

Review the output results:

```
DriveLetter Label      DiskSize(GB) FreeSpace(GB)
----------- -----      ------------ -------------
C:                     100          38
D:          Pagefiles  279          140
H:          Database   859          479
M:          TempDB     279          220
N:          Backup     659          410
```

PowerShell for SQL Server Part 4 completed.

Java for MongoDB
Part 1

MongoDB is document oriented database. It is classified as a **NoSQL** database.

The features of MongoDB include high performance, high availability and easy scalability.

It is handy to use Java programs to manipulate MongoDB, such as working on collections, documents in database.

This **Java for MongoDB** includes four parts:

Java for MongoDB Part 1, **MongoDB** collections by Java.
Java for MongoDB Part 2, **MongoDB** documents by Java.
Java for MongoDB Part 3, **MongoDB** maintenance by Java.
Java for MongoDB Part 4, **MapReduce** in MongoDB by Java.

Java for MongoDB Part 1 discusses using Java programs to:
create new collection in MongoDB
display all collections in MongoDB

(1) Create New Collection in MongoDB

Run the following Java code to create new database called demoDB.

It uses **createCollection()** method to create a new collection called demoCollection:

```java
import com.mongodb.client.MongoDatabase;
import com.mongodb.MongoClient;
import com.mongodb.MongoCredential;
public class createCollection {
public static void main(String atgs[]) {
MongoClient mongo = new MongoClient("localhost",
27017);
MongoCredential credential;
credential =
MongoCredential.createCredential("mongoDBUser",
"demoDB","password".toCharArray());
// access to database:
MongoDatabase database =
mongo.getDatabase("demoDB");
//create a new collection
database.createCollection("demoCollection");
    System.out.println("Collection created
successfully");
    }
}
```

From MongoDB shell to verify the newly created
collection, demoCollection:

```
> show dbs
demoDB 0.000GB
library 0.001GB
local 0.001GB
testDB 0.001GB
video 0.003GB

> use demoDB
switched to db demoDB

> show collections
demoCollection
```

(2) Using Java to Display All Collections in MongoDB

Run the following Java code to review all collections in a database.

The program uses **listCollectionNames()** method:

```java
import com.mongodb.client.MongoCollection;
import com.mongodb.client.MongoDatabase;
import com.mongodb.MongoClient;
import com.mongodb.MongoCredential;
public class showCollection {
   public static void main(String atgs[]) {
     MongoClient mongo = new MongoClient("localhost",
27017);
     MongoCredential credential;
     credential =
MongoCredential.createCredential("mongoDBUser","test
DB","password".toCharArray());
     MongoDatabase database =
mongo.getDatabase("testDB");
// call listCollectionNames() method:
for (String name : database.listCollectionNames()) {
   System.out.println(name);
   }
 }
}
```

The output results as the following:

system.profile
employees
mycollection
newcollection

From MongoDB shell to verify the results:

> use testDB
switched to db testDB

> show collections
employees
mycollection
newcollection
system.profile

Part 1 of Java for MongoDB is completed.

Java for MongoDB
Part 2

This part discusses using Java programs in MongoDB to:
insert document
update document
select all Documents from collection

(1) Using Java program to insert document into collection

The following program uses method called **insertOne()** to insert document into collection:

```java
import com.mongodb.client.MongoCollection;
import com.mongodb.client.MongoDatabase;

import org.bson.Document;
import com.mongodb.MongoClient;
import com.mongodb.MongoCredential;

public class InsertDocument {

public static void main(String atgs[]) {

MongoClient mongo = new MongoClient("localhost",
27017);
```

```java
MongoCredential credential;
credential = MongoCredential.createCredential
    ("mongoDBUser","demoDB","
    password".toCharArray());

MongoDatabase database =
mongo.getDatabase("demoDB");

MongoCollection<Document> collection =
database.getCollection("demoCollection");

//Using insertOne() method to insert document
Document document =
    new Document("title","Java for MongoDB")
.append("id",1)
.append("description","NoSQL database")
.append("likes", 180)
.append("url", "http://aleafboat.net/database/")
.append("by", "MongoDB Admin");
collection.insertOne(document);
System.out.println("document inserted
successfully");
    }
}
```

Verify the results from MongoDB shell:

```
> db.demoCollection.find().pretty()
{
"_id" : ObjectId("5a4517df72acc209e990bf65"),
"title" : "Java for MongoDB",
"id" : 1,
"description" : "NoSQL database",
"likes" : 180,
"url" : "http://aleafboat.net/database/",
"by" : "MongoDB Admin"
}
```

(2) Update Document in MongoDB

The following Java code uses **$set** to update "likes" to new value 219.

"searchQuery" searches the document need to be updated.

```java
import com.mongodb.BasicDBObject;
import com.mongodb.DB;
import com.mongodb.DBCollection;
import com.mongodb.DBCursor;
import com.mongodb.DBObject;
import com.mongodb.MongoClient;
public class updateDocument_old {
public static void main(String[] args)
throws Exception {
try
{
MongoClient mongoClient = new
MongoClient("localhost", 27017);
DB db = mongoClient.getDB("demoDB");
DBCollection coll = db.getCollection
                ("demoCollection");
BasicDBObject newDocument =
                new BasicDBObject();
newDocument.append("$set", new
BasicDBObject().append("likes", 219));
BasicDBObject searchQuery = new
BasicDBObject().append
                ("title","Java for MongoDB");
coll.update(searchQuery, newDocument);
}
catch (Exception e) {
System.err.println
( e.getClass().getName() + ": " + e.getMessage());
```

```
      }
    }
  }
```

Verify the result from MongoDB shell:


```
> db.demoCollection.find().pretty()
{
"_id" : ObjectId("5a4517df72acc209e990bf65"),
"title" : "Java for MongoDB",
"id" : 1,
"description" : "NoSQL database",
"likes" : 219,
"url" : "http://aleafboat.net/database/",
"by" : "MongoDB Admin"
}
```


(3) Select all Documents from Collection

The following Java code displays all documents in collection called newcollection.

It uses **getCollection()** method to retrieve collection, **find()** methods to find document and iterator() method to iterate in the cursor.


```
import com.mongodb.client.FindIterable;
import com.mongodb.client.MongoCollection;
import com.mongodb.client.MongoDatabase;
import java.util.Iterator;
import org.bson.Document;
import com.mongodb.MongoClient;
import com.mongodb.MongoCredential;
```

```java
public class SelectAllDocuments {
public static void main(String atgs[]) {
    MongoClient mongo = new
MongoClient("localhost", 27017);
MongoCredential credential;
   credential = MongoCredential.createCredential
("mongoDBUser","testDB","
password".toCharArray());

MongoDatabase database =
mongo.getDatabase("testDB");
MongoCollection<Document> collection =
    database.getCollection("newcollection");
    System.out.println
    ("Retrieve from newCollection successfully");


FindIterable<Document> iterDoc = collection.find();
int i =1;
Iterator it = iterDoc.iterator();
while (it.hasNext()) {
System.out.println(it.next());
i++;
    }
  }
}
```

The output shows three documents:

INFO: Opened connection [connectionId{localValue:2, serverValue:19}] to localhost:27017

Document{{_id=5a4276f7f2389464eb56bec2, title=MongoDB, description=MongoDB on testing server, by=MongoDB Admin, url=http://www.Aleafboat.net, tags=[MongoDB, NoSQL, database], likes=40.0}}

Document{{_id=5a427e0ef2389464eb56bec3, title=Java Programming, description=Object oriented program, by=http://Aleafboat.net, url=http://Aleafboat.net, tags=[Java, program, computer], likes=555.0, comments=[Document{{user=web searcher1, message=Hi, this is my comment, like=2.0}}]}}

Document{{_id=5a428d68f2389464eb56bec4, title=SQL Server 2016, description=SQL Server is relational database, by=SQL Server DBA, url=http://Aleafboat.net, tags=[SQL, RDBMS, database], popular=very, likes=500.0}}
BUILD SUCCESSFUL (total time: 1 second)

Part 2 of Java for MongoDB is completed.

Java for MongoDB
Part 3

This section discusses using Java program to delete all documents from a collection drop collection in database

(1) Using Java code to delete all documents from collection

The following Java code deletes all documents from collection called demoCollection.

Method called **remove()** is used to accomplish this task.

```java
import com.mongodb.BasicDBObject;
import com.mongodb.DB;
import com.mongodb.DBCollection;
import com.mongodb.DBCursor;
import com.mongodb.DBObject;
import com.mongodb.MongoClient;
public class DeleteAllDocs {
    public static void main(String[] args)throws Exception
{
```

```java
try
{
MongoClient mongoClient = new
MongoClient("localhost", 27017);
    DB db = mongoClient.getDB("demoDB");
    DBCollection coll =
db.getCollection("demoCollection");
    BasicDBObject doc = new BasicDBObject();
    coll.remove(doc);
    System.out.println("All documents deleted!");
    }
catch (Exception e) {
    System.err.println( e.getClass().getName() + ": " +
    e.getMessage());
      }
    }
}
```

(2) Drop collection in database

Using the following Java code to drop a collection from MongoDB database.

Using **getCollection()** method to identify the collection. Method called **drop()** is used to drop a collection.

```java
import com.mongodb.client.MongoCollection;
import com.mongodb.client.MongoDatabase;

import org.bson.Document;
import com.mongodb.MongoClient;
import com.mongodb.MongoCredential;
```

```java
public class DropCollection {

    public static void main(String atgs[]) {

        MongoClient mongo = new
        MongoClient("localhost", 27017);

        MongoCredential credential;
        credential = MongoCredential.createCredential
            ("mongoDBUser","demoDB","
            password".toCharArray());

        MongoDatabase database =
        mongo.getDatabase("demoDB");

        MongoCollection<Document> collection =
        database.getCollection("demoCollection");


        collection.drop();
        System.out.println("Collection hits dropped
        successfully...");
    }
}
```

Part 3 of Java for MongoDB completed.

Java for MongoDB Part 4 MapReduce I

MapReduce is a data processing technique that condenses large volumes of data into aggregated results.

MongoDB uses MapReduce command for map reduce operation. MapReduce is usually used for processing large volume of structured and unstructured big data sets with a parallel, distributed algorithm on a cluster.

A **MapReduce** program is composed of a **Map()** method and a **Reduce()** method.

The following example lists the mapReduce process by using Java program on a collection called weblogs in MongoDB.

MapReduce on weblogs collection steps:

(1) Insert documents into weblogs collection

The following commands insert documents into a collect called weblog:

```
db.weblogs.insert({user: "Mark", logon: new
Date(), site: "http://www.google.com"});
db.weblogs.insert({user: "Joe", logon: new
Date(), site: "http://aleafboat.com"});
db.weblogs.insert({user: "Mark", logon: new
Date(), site:
"http://www.aleafboat.net/database/"});
db.weblogs.insert({user: "John", logon: new
Date(), site: "http://www.amazon.com"});
db.weblogs.insert({user: "Joe", logon: new
Date(), site: "http://www.google.com"});
db.weblogs.insert({user: "Larry", logon: new
Date(), site: "http://www.aleafboat.net"});
db.weblogs.insert({user: "Mark", logon: new
Date(), site: "http://www.amazon.com"});
db.weblogs.insert({user: "John", logon: new
Date(), site: "http://www.aleafboat.net"});
db.weblogs.insert({user: "Tom", logon: new
Date(), site: "http://www.google.com"});
db.weblogs.insert({user: "Jimmy", logon: new
Date(), site: "http://www.homedepot.com"});
db.weblogs.insert({user: "Larry", logon: new
Date(), site: "http://www.aleafboat.net"});
```

(2) Java Program calls Map() and Reduce() Functions

The following Java program calls map function and
reduce function to complete MapReduce task.

```java
import com.mongodb.DB;
import com.mongodb.DBCollection;
import com.mongodb.DBObject;
import com.mongodb.MapReduceCommand;
import com.mongodb.MapReduceOutput;
import com.mongodb.MongoClient;
import java.net.UnknownHostException;

public class MapReduce_Weblogs {
    public static void main(String[] args) throws
UnknownHostException {
    MongoClient m1 = new MongoClient();
    DB db = m1.getDB("demoDB");
    DBCollection coll = db.getCollection("weblogs");
    // map function by site
    String weblogs_site_map = "function (){"
      + "emit(this.site, 1);" + "};";
    // reduce function
    String weblogs_reduce = "function(key, values) {"
      + "var res =0;"
      + "values.forEach(function(v){ res += 1});"
      + "return {count: res};"
      + "};";
    // MapReduce command by calling map and
reduce functions
    MapReduceCommand mapcommand = new
MapReduceCommand(coll, weblogs_site_map,
 weblogs_reduce,
 null, MapReduceCommand.OutputType.INLINE,
null);
    MapReduceOutput sites =
coll.mapReduce(mapcommand);
    for (DBObject o : sites.results()) {
      System.out.println(o.toString());
      }
    }
  }
```

(3) View output

The output results show number of logons on each site:

```
{ "_id" : "http://aleafboat.com" , "value" : 1.0}
{ "_id" : "http://www.aleafboat.net" , "value" :
{ "count" : 3.0}}
{ "_id" : "http://www.aleafboat.net/database/" ,
 "value" : 1.0}
{ "_id" : "http://www.amazon.com" , "value" :
{ "count" : 2.0}}
{ "_id" : "http://www.google.com" , "value" :
{ "count" : 3.0}}
{ "_id" : "http://www.homedepot.com" , "value"
 : 1.0}
```

BUILD SUCCESSFUL (total time: 1 second)

The aggregated results contain web logs for "http://www.google.com" with count value 3, and for "http://www.aleafboat.net" site with count value 3.

Part 4 Java for MongoDB is completed.

Java for MongoDB Part 5
MapReduce II

MapReduce is a data process which condense large volumes of data into useful aggregated results.

MongoDB supports MapReduce operation. The operation can write results to a collection or retune the results inline.

The example here uses Java class to perform MapReduce operation which contains Map function and Reduce function. The process will perform the string count in MongoDB document.

(1) Document in Collection

The following document contains text in a paragraph. Using MongoDB shell to check this collection:

```
> db.searchTest.find().pretty();
{
"_id" : ObjectId("5a95b07eb3645d8636a3646a"),
"title" : "CountWords",
"paragraph" : "This is a test to test Java MapReduce in
MongoDB which provides search test , speed test ,
MapReduce function test as well as the test to test the
performance."
}
```

(2) Java Program

The following Java code applies MongoDB **map** phase to the document in "paragraph" field to obtain key-value data. Then MongoDB applies the **reduce** phase to collect and condense the aggregated data.

This **MapReduce** process produces the count of each distinct string used in the document.

```
package mongodbtest;
import com.mongodb.DB;
import com.mongodb.DBCollection;
import com.mongodb.DBObject;
import com.mongodb.MapReduceCommand;
import com.mongodb.MapReduceOutput;
import com.mongodb.MongoClient;
import java.net.UnknownHostException;
public class MapReduce_CountWords {
public static void main(String[] args) throws
UnknownHostException {
```

```java
// create an instance of client and establish the
connection
MongoClient m1 = new MongoClient();
DB db = m1.getDB("demoDB");
DBCollection coll = db.getCollection("searchTest");
String Javamap = "function() {"
        + " var summary = this.paragraph;"
        + " if (summary) {"
        + " summary = summary.toLowerCase().split(' ')
          ;"
        + " for (var i = summary.length – 1; i >= 0; i–) {"
        + " if (summary[i]) {"
        + " emit(summary[i], 1);"
        + " } } }" + "};";
String Javareduce = "function( key, values ) {"
        + " var count = 0;"
        + " values.forEach(function(v) {"
        + " count +=v;});"
        + " return count"
        + "};";
// create the mapreduce command by calling map
and reduce functions
 MapReduceCommand mapcommand = new
MapReduceCommand(coll, Javamap, Javareduce,
null, MapReduceCommand.OutputType.INLINE,
null);
// invoke the mapreduce command
MapReduceOutput sites =
coll.mapReduce(mapcommand);

// print the results
for (DBObject o : sites.results()) {
System.out.println(o.toString());
    }
  }
}
```

(3) Output Results

The output of Java program as the following:

{ "_id" : "is" , "value" : 1.0}
{ "_id" : "java" , "value" : 1.0}
{ "_id" : "mapreduce" , "value" : 2.0}
{ "_id" : "mongodb" , "value" : 1.0}
{ "_id" : "performance." , "value" : 1.0}
{ "_id" : "provides" , "value" : 1.0}
{ "_id" : "search" , "value" : 1.0}
{ "_id" : "speed" , "value" : 1.0}
{ "_id" : "test" , "value" : 7.0}
{ "_id" : "the" , "value" : 2.0}
{ "_id" : "this" , "value" : 1.0}
{ "_id" : "to" , "value" : 2.0}
{ "_id" : "well" , "value" : 1.0}
{ "_id" : "which" , "value" : 1.0}

BUILD SUCCESSFUL (total time: 1 seconds)

The above map reduce results show that word "test" has been used 7 times in the document.
Word "mapreduce" has been used 2 times.

Part 5 Java for MongoDB is completed.

MongoDB Aggregation

Aggregation operations group values from multiple documents together, and can perform a variety of operations on the grouped data to return a single result.

MongoDB uses **Aggregate()** method to process a count of the number of documents.

The following section lists MongoDB aggregate process by using web log file as example.

(1) JSON file

JSON (Java Script Object Notation) file is used in MongoDB to support all the basic data types, including numbers, strings, boolean values and arrays.

The example of JSON file here is called website.json

{"_id" : 1, "url" : "www.google.com", "date" :
"2017-12-20", "trash_time" : 6 }
{"_id" : 2, "url" : "www.aleafboat.com", "date" :
"2017-12-19", "trash_time" : 5 }
{"_id" : 3, "url" : "www.aleafboat.com", "date" :
"2017-12-21", "trash_time" : 2 }
{"_id" : 4, "url" : "www.amazon.com", "date" :
"2017-12-23", "trash_time" : 10 }
{"_id" : 5, "url" : "www.walmart.com", "date" :
"2018-01-11", "trash_time" : 6 }
{"_id" : 6, "url" : "www.ebay.com", "date" :
"2017-12-28", "trash_time" : 3 }
{"_id" : 7, "url" : "www.google.com", "date" :
"2018-01-02", "trash_time" : 9 }
{"_id" : 8, "url" : "www.amazon.com", "date" :
"2018-01-16", "trash_time" : 4 }
{"_id" : 9, "url" : "www.google.com", "date" :
"2018-01-20", "trash_time" : 11 }
{"_id" : 10, "url" : "www.aleafboat.com", "date" :
"2018-01-22", "trash_time" : 1 }

(2) Import JSON File

The following command import json file to MongoDB collection called: webaccess

$ mongoimport –db demoDB –collection webaccess –file ~/Downloads/MongoDB/exercise/website.json

2018-02-28T09:59:36.638-0500 connected to: localhost
2018-02-28T09:59:37.184-0500 imported 10 documents

(3) Check MongoDB Collection

> *use demoDB*
switched to db demoDB

> *db.webaccess.find();*

{ "_id" : 1, "url" : "www.google.com", "date" : "2017-12-20", "trash_time" : 6 }
{ "_id" : 2, "url" : "www.aleafboat.com", "date" : "2017-12-19", "trash_time" : 5 }
{ "_id" : 3, "url" : "www.aleafboat.com", "date" : "2017-12-21", "trash_time" : 2 }
{ "_id" : 4, "url" : "www.amazon.com", "date" : "2017-12-23", "trash_time" : 10 }
{ "_id" : 5, "url" : "www.walmart.com", "date" : "2018-01-11", "trash_time" : 6 }
{ "_id" : 6, "url" : "www.ebay.com", "date" : "2017-12-28", "trash_time" : 3 }
{ "_id" : 7, "url" : "www.google.com", "date" : "2018-01-02", "trash_time" : 9 }
{ "_id" : 8, "url" : "www.amazon.com", "date" : "2018-01-16", "trash_time" : 4 }
{ "_id" : 9, "url" : "www.google.com", "date" : "2018-01-20", "trash_time" : 11 }
{ "_id" : 10, "url" : "www.aleafboat.com", "date" : "2018-01-22", "trash_time" : 1 }

(4) Using MongoDB aggregate to find the number of visit in each site

> *db.webaccess.aggregate({ $group : {_id : "$url",*
visit_time : {$sum : 1}}});

```
{ "_id" : "www.walmart.com", "visit_time" : 1 }
{ "_id" : "www.amazon.com", "visit_time" : 2 }
{ "_id" : "www.aleafboat.com", "visit_time" : 3 }
{ "_id" : "www.ebay.com", "visit_time" : 1 }
{ "_id" : "www.google.com", "visit_time" : 3 }
```

Above command uses Group function to count the number of visit in each site.

(5) Sort aggregate Results

> *db.webaccess.aggregate({ $group : {_id : "$url",*
visit_time : {$sum : 1}}}, {$sort : {visit_time : -1}});

{ "_id" : "www.aleafboat.com", "visit_time" : 3 }
{ "_id" : "www.google.com", "visit_time" : 3 }
{ "_id" : "www.amazon.com", "visit_time" : 2 }
{ "_id" : "www.walmart.com", "visit_time" : 1 }
{ "_id" : "www.ebay.com", "visit_time" : 1 }

Above results show that sorted aggregate results in
descending order to list the high visit number on the top.

Cassandra Development
Part 1

Apache Cassandra is a distributed **NoSQL** database management system designed to handle large amounts of data across multiple servers. It provides high availability with no single point of failure.

Cassandra offers robust support for clusters spanning multiple datacenters, with asynchronous masterless replication allowing low latency operations for all clients. Every **Cassandra** node in the cluster has the same role. Data is distributed across the cluster.

Cassandra Development Part 1 lists using Java API to connect to Cassandra database and create Keyspace in Cassandra cluster.

(1) Connect to Cassandra

The following Java code uses the **execute()** method in session class connect to **keyspace** "cassdev" in Cassandra cluster. **Cassandra cluster** holds the sum total of all the nodes located in each datacenter.

```java
import com.datastax.driver.core.Cluster;
import com.datastax.driver.core.Host;
import com.datastax.driver.core.Metadata;
import com.datastax.driver.core.Session;
import static java.lang.System.out;
public class cassandraConnect
{
        private static Cluster cluster;
        private static Session session;
    public static void main(String[] args) {
        cassandraConnect cassandraconnect = new
cassandraConnect();
        cassandraconnect.connect("127.0.0.1");
        session.execute("USE cassdev");
        System.out.println("Keyspace is in use.");
        session.close();
        cluster.close();
    }
    public void connect(final String node) {
        cluster =
Cluster.builder().addContactPoint(node).build();
        session = cluster.connect();
        Metadata metadata = cluster.getMetadata();
        System.out.println("Connect to cluster: " +
metadata.getClusterName());
```

```
for (Host host: metadata.getAllHosts()) {
    System.out.println(String.format("Data Center: "
+
    host.getDatacenter() + ", \n"
    + "Host: " +
    host.getAddress() + ", \n"
    + "Rack: " +
    host.getRack() + ", \n"
    + "Cassandra Version: " +
    host.getCassandraVersion() + ", \n"
    + "State: " +
    host.getState() + ", \n"
    + "Schema Version: " +
    host.getSchemaVersion() + ", \n"
    + "Class: " +
    host.getClass()
    ));
  }
 }
}
```

The output shows the connected cassandra cluster information:

```
Connect to cluster: Test Cluster
Data Center: datacenter1,
Host: /127.0.0.1,
Rack: rack1,
Cassandra Version: 3.0.9,
State: UP,
Schema Version: 40e3eaab-6080-31b1-aa1a-147d938090aa,
Class: class com.datastax.driver.core.Host
Keyspace is in use.
-----------------------------------------------------
BUILD SUCCESS
-----------------------------------------------------
```

(2) Create Keyspace

A **keyspace** in Cassandra is a top-level namespace that defines data replication on nodes. Keyspace holds together all column families of a design.

The following Java code uses **createSchema()** method to create a new keyspace and a new table in Cassandra database:

```
import com.datastax.driver.core.Cluster;
import com.datastax.driver.core.Host;
import com.datastax.driver.core.Metadata;
import com.datastax.driver.core.ResultSet;
import com.datastax.driver.core.Session;
public class cassandraCreateKeyspace {
    private static Cluster cluster;
    private static Session session;
public static void main(String[] args) {
    cassandraCreateKeyspace cassandrakeyspace = new
cassandraCreateKeyspace();
    cassandrakeyspace.connect("127.0.0.1");
    // create new Keyspace and table:
    cassandrakeyspace.createSchema();
    // close connection:
    cassandrakeyspace.close();
}
    public void connect(final String node) {
        cluster =
        Cluster.builder().addContactPoint(node).build();
        session = cluster.connect();
    }
```

```java
// this method creates new keyspace and new table:
public void createSchema() {
    session.execute("CREATE KEYSPACE IF NOT
EXISTS dev WITH replication " +
    "=
{'class':'SimpleStrategy','replication_factor':1};");
    System.out.println(" ");
    System.out.println("New KeySpace is created.");
    session.execute("CREATE TABLE IF NOT EXISTS
dev.userList (" +
    "user_id int PRIMARY KEY, " +
    "user_name text, " +
"user_rating int" +
");");
    System.out.println("New table is created.");
}
public void close() {
    cluster.close();
    session.close();
}
}
```

The following is the output screenshot:

```
New KeySpace is created.
Table is created.
-------------------------------------------------
BUILD SUCCESS
-------------------------------------------------
```

Cassandra Development Part 1 is completed.

Cassandra Development
Part 2

Data Manipulation

Cassandra Development Part 2 discusses using **Java** program to manipulate data in Cassandra, such as insert, update and delete data.

Cassandra Query Language (CQL) is used in Java code to access Cassandra database. **CQL** is the primary language to interact with Cassandra. **CQL** offers a model close to traditional **SQL** in the sense that data is put in tables containing rows and columns.

(1) Insert Data

The following Java code uses **insertData()** method to insert new data into table located in cassandra keyspace. Using **query()** method to retrieve data from table.

```
import com.datastax.driver.core.Cluster;
import com.datastax.driver.core.ResultSet;
import com.datastax.driver.core.Row;
import com.datastax.driver.core.Session;
import java.io.PrintStream;
public class cassandraInsertData {
    private static Cluster cluster;
    private static Session session;
```

```java
public static void main(String[] args) {
    cassandraInsertData cassandrainsert = new
cassandraInsertData();
    // connect cluster:
    cassandrainsert.connect("127.0.0.1");
    // connect keyspace:
    Session session = cluster.connect("dev");
    cassandrainsert.insertData();
    cassandrainsert.query();
    // close connection:
    cassandrainsert.close();
    }
public void insertData() {
    session.execute("INSERT INTO
dev.userTab(name,email,rating) " +
    " VALUES('Rick','rick@aleafboat.net',30);");
    System.out.println("New data is inserted in table.");
    System.out.println(" ");
    }
public void connect(final String node) {
    cluster =
Cluster.builder().addContactPoint(node).build();
    session = cluster.connect();
    }
public void query() {
    ResultSet resultSet = session.execute("SELECT *
FROM dev.userTab;");
    System.out.println(String.format("%-30s\t%-5s",
"Email","Rating"));
    for (Row row : resultSet) {
        System.out.println(String.format("%-30s\t%d",
row.getString("email"), row.getInt("rating")));
    }
    }
public void close() {
    cluster.close();
    session.close();
    }
}
```

The output shows all users in the table:

```
New data is inserted in table.

Email                           Rating
jackson@aleafboat.net           33
dacan@aleafboat.net             41
rick@aleafboat.net              30
lisa@aleafboat.net              48
------------------------------------
BUILD SUCCESS
------------------------------------
```

(2) Update data

The following Java code uses **updateData()** method to update data in table located in cassandra keyspace. Using **query()** method to retrieve data from table.

```java
import com.datastax.driver.core.Cluster;
import com.datastax.driver.core.ResultSet;
import com.datastax.driver.core.Row;
import com.datastax.driver.core.Session;
import com.datastax.driver.core.querybuilder.Clause;
import com.datastax.driver.core.querybuilder.QueryBuilder;
import com.datastax.driver.core.querybuilder.Update;
import java.io.PrintStream;
public class cassandraUpdate {
    private static Cluster cluster;
    private static Session session;
```

```java
public static void main(String[] args) {
    cassandraUpdate cassandrapdate = new
cassandraUpdate();

cassandrapdate.connect("127.0.0.1");
Session session = cluster.connect("dev");
cassandrapdate.updateData();
// retrieve data:
cassandrapdate.query();
cassandrapdate.close();
 }
 public void updateData() {
Update.Where update =
 QueryBuilder.update("dev","userTab")
     .with(QueryBuilder.set("rating",44))
     .where(QueryBuilder.eq("name","Lisa"));
session.execute(update);
System.out.println("Data is updated.");
System.out.println(" ");
 }
 public void connect(final String node) {
cluster = Cluster.builder().addContactPoint(node).build();
session = cluster.connect();
 }
 public void query() {
ResultSet resultSet = session.execute("SELECT * FROM
     dev.userTab;");
System.out.println(String.format("%-30s\t%-5s",
"Email","Rating"));
for (Row row : resultSet) {
  System.out.println(String.format("%-30s\t%d",
row.getString("email"), row.getInt("rating")));
   }
}
public void close() {
 cluster.close();
 session.close();
   }
 }
```

The output shows all users in table userTab:

```
Data is updated.

Email                          Rating
jackson@aleafboat.net          33
dacan@aleafboat.net            41
rick@aleafboat.net             30
lisa@aleafboat.net             44
----------------------------------------------
BUILD SUCCESS
----------------------------------------------
```

(3) Delete data

The following Java code uses **deleteData()** method to delete data from table located in cassandra keyspace. Using **query()** method to retrieve data from table.

```java
import com.datastax.driver.core.Cluster;
import com.datastax.driver.core.ResultSet;
import com.datastax.driver.core.Row;
import com.datastax.driver.core.Session;
import com.datastax.driver.core.querybuilder.Clause;
import com.datastax.driver.core.querybuilder.QueryBuilder;
import com.datastax.driver.core.querybuilder.Update;
import java.io.PrintStream;
public class cassandraDelete {
    private static Cluster cluster;
    private static Session session;
```

```java
public static void main(String[] args) {
    cassandraDelete cassandradelete = new
cassandraDelete();
    cassandradelete.connect("127.0.0.1");
    Session session = cluster.connect("dev");
//delete data
cassandradelete.deleteData();
// retrieve data:
cassandradelete.query();
cassandradelete.close();
 }
public void deleteData() {
    session.execute("DELETE FROM dev.userTab
WHERE name='Lisa';");
    System.out.println("Data is deleted.");
 }
public void connect(final String node) {
    cluster =
Cluster.builder().addContactPoint(node).build();
    session = cluster.connect();
 }
public void query() {
    ResultSet resultSet = session.execute("SELECT *
FROM dev.userTab;");
    System.out.println(String.format("%-30s\t%-5s",
"Email","Rating"));
    for (Row row : resultSet) {
        System.out.println(String.format("%-30s\t%d",
row.getString("email"), row.getInt("rating")));
    }
 }
public void close() {
    cluster.close();
    session.close();
 }
}
```

The query output shows one user record is deleted.

```
Data is deleted.

Email                           Rating
jackson@aleafboat.net           33
dacan@aleafboat.net             41
rick@aleafboat.net              30
-------------------------------------------------
BUILD SUCCESS
-------------------------------------------------
```

Cassandra Development Part 2 is completed.

Cassandra Development
Part 3

Cassandra Collections

Cassandra has three collection data types which can handle multiple data elements. Collections can group and store data together in a column.

Three types of collections are:
SET,
LIST,
MAP.

I. SET

A set consists of a group of elements with unique values. Use Set data type to store data that has a many-to-one relationship with another column.

(1) Create Cassandra Set and Insert Data

The following Java codes create a new table and insert data. Class column is a SET collection which uses **set<varchar>**.

CQL query used to create table is:

> *CREATE TABLE IF NOT EXISTS dev.students*
> *(name text,*
> *class set<varchar>,*
> *PRIMARY KEY (name));*

The Java codes to create SET collection listed as the following:

```
import com.datastax.driver.core.Cluster;
import com.datastax.driver.core.ResultSet;
import com.datastax.driver.core.Row;

import com.datastax.driver.core.Session;public class
cassandraCreateSet {
  private static Cluster cluster;
  private static Session session;


public static void main(String[] args) {
    cassandraCreateSet cassandraset = new
cassandraCreateSet();
    cassandraset.connect("127.0.0.1");
    Session session = cluster.connect("dev");
    cassandraset.createTable();
    cassandraset.insertData();
    cassandraset.query();
    cassandraset.close();
    }
```

```java
public void createTable() {
    session.execute("CREATE TABLE IF NOT
            EXISTS dev.students (" +
    "name text, " +
    "class set<varchar>," +
    "PRIMARY KEY (name));");
System.out.println("New table is created in
    keyspace dev.");
System.out.println(" ");
}

public void insertData() {
    session.execute("INSERT INTO
            dev.students(name,class) " +
    " VALUES('Jeff',{'NoSQL','Java','MongoDB'});");
    System.out.println
                ("New data is inserted in table.");
    System.out.println(" ");
    }

public void query() {
    ResultSet resultSet = session.execute
            ("SELECT * FROM dev.students;");
    System.out.println(resultSet.all());
    }

public void connect(final String node) {
    cluster = Cluster.builder().addContactPoint(node)
                .build();
    session = cluster.connect();
    }

public void close() {
    cluster.close();
    session.close();
    }
}
```

The output from Java codes listed as the following:

New table is created in keyspace dev.
New data is inserted in table.
[Row[Jeff, [Java, MongoDB, NoSQL]]]

BUILD SUCCESS

----

(2) Update Set

The following Java code performs update data in SET. New value 'MySQL' is added.


```
import com.datastax.driver.core.Cluster;
import com.datastax.driver.core.ResultSet;
import com.datastax.driver.core.Row;
import com.datastax.driver.core.Session;
import
com.datastax.driver.core.querybuilder.QueryBuilder;

import com.datastax.driver.core.querybuilder.Update;

public class cassandraUpdateSet {
    private static Cluster cluster;
    private static Session session;
public static void main(String[] args) {
    cassandraUpdateSet cassandrapdateet = new
cassandraUpdateSet();
    cassandrapdateet.connect("127.0.0.1");
    Session session = cluster.connect("dev");
    cassandrapdateet.updateData();
```

```java
        cassandrapdateet.query();
        cassandrapdateet.close();
    }
    public void updateData() {
        session.execute("UPDATE dev.students SET class =
class + {'MySQL'} WHERE name = 'Jeff';");
        System.out.println("Data is updated.");
        System.out.println(" ");
    }
    public void query() {
        ResultSet resultSet = session.execute("SELECT *
FROM dev.students;");
System.out.println(resultSet.all());
    }
    public void connect(final String node) {
        cluster =
Cluster.builder().addContactPoint(node).build();
        session = cluster.connect();
    }
    public void close() {
        cluster.close();
        session.close();
    }
}
```

The above Java codes added new class 'MySQL' into SET collection.

II. LIST

A list is much like a set.
However a List can store duplicated values. List stores elements in a particular order and inserted and retrieved according to an index value.

(1) Create List and Insert Data

The following Java codes create a new table called "cars" and insert data. Model column is List data type which uses **list<text>**.

CQL query used to create table is:

CREATE TABLE IF NOT EXISTS dev.cars
(car text,
model list<text>,
PRIMARY KEY (car));

The Java codes creating new LIST collection as the following:

```
import com.datastax.driver.core.Cluster;
import com.datastax.driver.core.ResultSet;
import com.datastax.driver.core.Row;
import com.datastax.driver.core.Session;
public class cassandraListCreate {
    private static Cluster cluster;
    private static Session session;
public static void main(String[] args) {
    cassandraListCreate cassandralist = new
cassandraListCreate();
    cassandralist.connect("127.0.0.1");
    Session session = cluster.connect("dev");
    cassandralist.createTable();
    cassandralist.insertData();
    cassandralist.query();
    cassandralist.close();
    }
```

```java
public void createTable() {
    session.execute("CREATE TABLE IF NOT EXISTS dev.cars (" +
    "car text, " +
    "model list<text>," +
    "PRIMARY KEY (car));");
    System.out.println("New table is created
    in keyspace dev.");
    }

public void insertData() {
    session.execute("INSERT INTO
        dev.cars(car,model) " +
    " VALUES('Mazda',['RX-7','CX-3','MX-5']);");
    System.out.println("New data is inserted
        in table.");
    System.out.println(" ");
    }

public void query() {
    ResultSet resultSet = session.execute
        ("SELECT * FROM dev.cars;");
    System.out.println(resultSet.all());
    }

public void connect(final String node) {
    cluster =
Cluster.builder().addContactPoint(node).build();
    session = cluster.connect();
    }

public void close() {
    cluster.close();
    session.close();
    }
 }
```

The output shows three new car models added:
––––––––––––
New table is created in keyspace dev.
New data is inserted in table.
[Row[Mazda, [RX-7, CX-3, MX-5]]]
––––––––––––
BUILD SUCCESS
––––––––––––

(2) Update List

The following Java codes perform the update data in LIST collection. New car model is added.

```
import com.datastax.driver.core.Cluster;
import com.datastax.driver.core.ResultSet;
import com.datastax.driver.core.Session;
public class cassandraListUpdate {
    private static Cluster cluster;
    private static Session session;
public static void main(String[] args) {
    cassandraListUpdate cassandraistupdate = new
cassandraListUpdate();
    cassandraistupdate.connect("127.0.0.1");
    Session session = cluster.connect("dev");
    cassandraistupdate.updateData();
    cassandraistupdate.query();
    cassandraistupdate.close();
    }
public void updateData() {
    session.execute("UPDATE dev.cars SET model =
model + ['Mazda6'] WHERE car = 'Mazda';");
    System.out.println("Data is updated.");
    System.out.println(" ");
    }
```

```
public void query() {
    ResultSet resultSet = session.execute("SELECT *
FROM dev.cars;");
    System.out.println(resultSet.all());
    }
public void connect(final String node) {
    cluster =
Cluster.builder().addContactPoint(node).build();
    session = cluster.connect();
    }
public void close() {
    cluster.close();
    session.close();
    }
}
```

The output from Java code as the following. New value
"Mazda6" is added:
— — — — — — — — — — — — — —
Data is updated.
[Row[Mazda, [RX-7, CX-3, MX-5, Mazda6]]]
— — — — — — — — — — — — — —
BUILD SUCCESS
— — — — — — — — — — — — — —-

III. MAP

A MAP stores **key-value pair** data. It relates one item to
another. For each key, only one value may exist, duplicates
cannot be stored. MAP collection can store timestamp-
related data in table.

(1) Create Map

The following Java codes create a new table. 'Registration'
column is a MAP data type which uses **map<varchar,date>**.

CQL query used to create map table as the following:

CREATE TABLE IF NOT EXISTS dev.usersReg
(user_id text,
user_name text,
registration map<varchar,date>,
PRIMARY KEY (user_id));

The following are Java codes to created Cassandra table with MAP data type:

```
import com.datastax.driver.core.Cluster;
import com.datastax.driver.core.ResultSet;
import com.datastax.driver.core.Session;
public class cassandraMapCreate {
    private static Cluster cluster;
    private static Session session;
public static void main(String[] args) {
    cassandraMapCreate cassandramap = new
cassandraMapCreate();
    cassandramap.connect("127.0.0.1");
    Session session = cluster.connect("dev");
    cassandramap.createTable();
    cassandramap.insertData();
    cassandramap.query();
    cassandramap.close();
    }
public void createTable() {
    session.execute("CREATE TABLE IF NOT EXISTS
dev.usersReg (" +
    "user_id text, " +
    "user_name text, " +
    "registration map<varchar,date>," +
    "PRIMARY KEY (user_id));");
    System.out.println("New table is created in keyspace
```

```java
dev.");
        System.out.println(" ");
    }
public void insertData() {
        session.execute("INSERT INTO
dev.usersReg(user_id,user_name, registration) " +
        " VALUES('1005','Joe Smith', {'Apache
Cassandra':'2016-10-22'});");
        System.out.println("New data is inserted in table.");
        System.out.println(" ");
    }
public void query() {
    ResultSet resultSet = session.execute("SELECT
user_id, user_name, registration FROM   dev.usersReg;");
        System.out.println(resultSet.all());
    }
public void connect(final String node) {
        cluster =
Cluster.builder().addContactPoint(node).build();
        session = cluster.connect();
    }
public void close() {
        cluster.close();
        session.close();
    }
}
```

The output as the following:

_____

New table is created in keyspace dev.
New data is inserted in table.
[Row[1005, Joe Smith, {Apache Cassandra=2016-10-22}]]
_____

BUILD SUCCESS

_____

(2) Update Map

The following Java codes perform data update in MAP collection. New value 'Big data' is added.

```
import com.datastax.driver.core.Cluster;
import com.datastax.driver.core.ResultSet;
import com.datastax.driver.core.Session;
public class cassandraMapUpdate {
    private static Cluster cluster;
    private static Session session;
public static void main(String[] args) {
    cassandraMapUpdate cassandramapupdate = new
cassandraMapUpdate();
        cassandramapupdate.connect("127.0.0.1");
        Session session = cluster.connect("dev");
        cassandramapupdate.updateData();
        cassandramapupdate.query();
        cassandramapupdate.close();
    }
public void updateData() {
    session.execute("UPDATE dev.usersReg SET
registration = registration + {'Big data': '2017-02-11'} " +
    " WHERE user_id = '1005';");
    System.out.println("Data is updated.");
    System.out.println(" ");
    }
public void query() {
    ResultSet resultSet = session.execute("SELECT
user_id, user_name, registration FROM dev.usersReg;");
    System.out.println(resultSet.all());
    }
public void connect(final String node) {
    cluster =
Cluster.builder().addContactPoint(node).build();
```

```
        session = cluster.connect();
    }
public void close() {
    cluster.close();
    session.close();
    }
}
```

The output from the Java codes shows new key-value pair is added in Map:

- - - - - - - - - - - - - - - - - - - -
Data is updated.
[Row[1005, Joe Smith, {Apache Cassandra=
2016-10-22, Big data=2017-02-11}]]
- - - - - - - - - - - - - - - - - - - -
BUILD SUCCESS

Cassandra Development Part 3 is completed.

Cassandra Development
Part 4

Custom Index

Starting from Apache Cassandra version 3.4 SASI index (SSTable Attached Secondary Index) can be used to create custom index.

Custom index can specially help to search data in non-collection column or collection column.

Three custom index modes are:

PREFIX,
CONTAINS,
SPARSE.

(1) Custom Index using PREFIX

When Prefix index is created in Cassandra data table, the data can be easily searched by using LIKE keyword in the query. Such as using LIKE 'M%'.

The following example works in Cassandra **CQLSH** environment.

(1.1) Select Data from Table

cqlsh:dev> *select * from usersreg;*

user_id | registration | user_name
———+———————————————-+———
1005 | {'Apache Cassandra': 2016-10-22, 'Big data': 2017-02-11} | Joe Smith
1006 | {'NoSQL': 2017-01-10} | Michael Jones
(2 rows)

(1.2) Create Custom Index

cqlsh:dev> *CREATE CUSTOM INDEX user_name_idx*
        ON usersReg (user_name)
        USING
'org.apache.cassandra.index.sasi.SASIIndex'
        WITH OPTIONS = { 'mode' : 'PREFIX',
        'analyzer_class' :
'org.apache.cassandra.index.sasi.analyzer.
        NonTokenizingAnalyzer',
        'case_sensitive' : 'false'};

Review the newly created custom index:

cqlsh:dev> *describe usersReg;*

```
CREATE TABLE dev.usersreg (
user_id text PRIMARY KEY,
registration map<text, date>,
user_name text
) WITH bloom_filter_fp_chance = 0.01
AND caching = {'keys': 'ALL', 'rows_per_partition':
'NONE'}
AND comment = "
AND compaction = {'class':
'org.apache.cassandra.db.compaction.SizeTieredCompa
ctionStrategy', 'max_threshold': '32', 'min_threshold':
'4'}
AND compression = {'chunk_length_in_kb': '64', 'class':
'org.apache.cassandra.io.compress.LZ4Compressor'}
AND crc_check_chance = 1.0
AND dclocal_read_repair_chance = 0.1
AND default_time_to_live = 0
AND gc_grace_seconds = 864000
AND max_index_interval = 2048
AND memtable_flush_period_in_ms = 0
AND min_index_interval = 128
AND read_repair_chance = 0.0
AND speculative_retry = '99PERCENTILE';
    CREATE CUSTOM INDEX user_name_idx ON
    dev.usersreg (user_name) USING
    'org.apache.cassandra.index.sasi.SASIIndex' WITH
    OPTIONS = {'mode': 'PREFIX', 'analyzer_class':
    'org.apache.cassandra.index.sasi.analyzer.NonToke
    nizingAnalyzer', 'case_sensitive': 'false'};
```

(1.3) Search Data by New Index

The query uses LIKE search condition in WHERE clause.

cqlsh:dev> *SELECT * FROM usersReg WHERE user_name LIKE 'J%';*

```
user_id | registration | user_name
———+————————————————————-+————
1005 | {'Apache Cassandra': 2016-10-22, 'Big data': 2017-02-11}
| Joe Smith
(1 rows)
```

(2) Custom Index using CONTAINS

When CONTAINS index is created in Cassandra table, the data can be easily searched by using LIKE keyword in the query, such as **LIKE '%m%'**.

(2.1) Create New Index

cqlsh:dev>*CREATE CUSTOM INDEX instructor_name_idx*
        ON usersReg (user_name)
        USING
'org.apache.cassandra.index.sasi.SASIIndex'
        WITH OPTIONS = { 'mode' : 'CONTAINS',
        'analyzer_class' :
    'org.apache.cassandra.index.sasi.analyzer.
    NonTokenizingAnalyzer',
        'case_sensitive' : 'false' };

Review the newly created index:

cqlsh:dev> *describe usersReg;*

CREATE TABLE dev.usersreg (
user_id text PRIMARY KEY,
registration map<text, date>,
user_name text
) WITH bloom_filter_fp_chance = 0.01
AND caching = {'keys': 'ALL', 'rows_per_partition': 'NONE'}
AND comment = ''
AND compaction = {'class':
'org.apache.cassandra.db.compaction.SizeTieredCompactio
nStrategy', 'max_threshold': '32', 'min_threshold': '4'}
AND compression = {'chunk_length_in_kb': '64', 'class':
'org.apache.cassandra.io.compress.LZ4Compressor'}
AND crc_check_chance = 1.0
AND dclocal_read_repair_chance = 0.1
AND default_time_to_live = 0
AND gc_grace_seconds = 864000
AND max_index_interval = 2048
AND memtable_flush_period_in_ms = 0
AND min_index_interval = 128
AND read_repair_chance = 0.0
AND speculative_retry = '99PERCENTILE';
CREATE CUSTOM INDEX instructor_name_idx
ON dev.usersreg (user_name) USING
'org.apache.cassandra.index.sasi.SASIIndex' WITH
OPTIONS = {'mode': 'CONTAINS', 'analyzer_class':
'org.apache.cassandra.index.sasi.analyzer.NonTokenizingAn
alyzer', 'case_sensitive': 'false'};

(2.2) Search Data by using Index

The query uses LIKE search condition in WHERE clause.

cqlsh:dev> *SELECT * FROM usersReg WHERE user_name LIKE '%m%';*

```
user_id | registration | user_name
———+————————————————————-+—————
1005 | {'Apache Cassandra': 2016-10-22, 'Big data': 2017-02-11}
| Joe Smith
1006 | {'NoSQL': 2017-01-10} | Michael Jones
(2 rows)
```

(3) Custom Index using SPARSE

The SPARSE index can help to improve performance of querying large amount od numeric data such as timestamps.

(3.1) Select Data from Table

cqlsh:dev> *select * from visitors;*

```
name | email | visit_date
———+————————+————
Joe | joe@aleafboat.net | 2016-11-19
Rick | rick@aleafboat.net | 2017-01-10
Michael | mike@aleafboat.net | 2016-10-26
(3 rows)
```

(3.2) Create Custom Index

cqlsh:dev> *CREATE CUSTOM INDEX visitor_date_idx*
ON dev.visitors (visit_date)
USING
'org.apache.cassandra.index.sasi.SASIIndex'
WITH OPTIONS = {'mode': 'SPARSE'};

cqlsh:dev> *describe visitors;*


```
CREATE TABLE dev.visitors (
name text PRIMARY KEY,
email text,
visit_date date
) WITH bloom_filter_fp_chance = 0.01
AND caching = {'keys': 'ALL', 'rows_per_partition': 'NONE'}
AND comment = "
AND compaction = {'class':
'org.apache.cassandra.db.compaction.SizeTieredCompactio
nStrategy', 'max_threshold': '32', 'min_threshold': '4'}
AND compression = {'chunk_length_in_kb': '64', 'class':
'org.apache.cassandra.io.compress.LZ4Compressor'}
AND crc_check_chance = 1.0
AND dclocal_read_repair_chance = 0.1
AND default_time_to_live = 0
AND gc_grace_seconds = 864000
AND max_index_interval = 2048
AND memtable_flush_period_in_ms = 0
AND min_index_interval = 128
AND read_repair_chance = 0.0
AND speculative_retry = '99PERCENTILE';
CREATE CUSTOM INDEX visitor_date_idx
ON dev.visitors (visit_date) USING
'org.apache.cassandra.index.sasi.SASIIndex'
WITH OPTIONS = {'mode': 'SPARSE'};
```

(3.3) Select Data by using Index

cqlsh:dev> *SELECT * FROM visitors WHERE visit_date <'2017-01-01';*

name | email | visit_date
———+————————+————
Joe | joe@aleafboat.net | 2016-11-19
Michael | mike@aleafboat.net | 2016-10-26
(2 rows)

(4) Index on Map Collection using KEYS

Create custom index on MAP collection by using KEYS can help to search **key-value** pair data.

In the following example registration column is MAP collection containing <text, date>.

(4.1) Select from Table

cqlsh:dev> *SELECT user_id, user_name, registration FROM dev.usersReg ;*

user_id | user_name | registration
———+——————+———————————————
1006 | Michael Jones | {'Big data': 2017-02-11, 'NoSQL': 2017-01-10}
1007 | Jimmy Smith | {'Cassandra': 2017-03-28}
(2 rows)

(4.2) Create Index

cqlsh:dev> **CREATE INDEX IF NOT EXISTS**
reg_map_idx
ON dev.usersReg (KEYS(registration));

Review the newly created index:

cqlsh:dev> *describe usersreg;*

```
CREATE TABLE dev.usersreg (
user_id text PRIMARY KEY,
registration map<text, date>,
user_name text
) WITH bloom_filter_fp_chance = 0.01
    AND caching = {'keys': 'ALL', 'rows_per_partition':
    'NONE'}
AND comment = "
AND compaction = {'class':
'org.apache.cassandra.db.compaction.SizeTieredCompa
ctionStrategy', 'max_threshold': '32', 'min_threshold':
'4'}
AND compression = {'chunk_length_in_kb': '64', 'class':
'org.apache.cassandra.io.compress.LZ4Compressor'}
AND crc_check_chance = 1.0
AND dclocal_read_repair_chance = 0.1
AND default_time_to_live = 0
AND gc_grace_seconds = 864000
AND max_index_interval = 2048
AND memtable_flush_period_in_ms = 0
AND min_index_interval = 128
AND read_repair_chance = 0.0
AND speculative_retry = '99PERCENTILE';
CREATE CUSTOM INDEX user_name_idx_2 ON
dev.usersreg (user_name) USING
'org.apache.cassandra.index.sasi.SASIIndex' WITH
OPTIONS = {'mode': 'CONTAINS', 'analyzer_class':
```

'org.apache.cassandra.index.sasi.analyzer.NonTokenizin
gAnalyzer', 'case_sensitive': 'false'};
CREATE INDEX reg_map_idx ON dev.usersreg
(keys(registration));

(4.3) Select data by using CONTAINS KEY keyword

cqlsh:dev> *SELECT user_id, user_name, registration*
       FROM dev.usersReg
       WHERE registration
       CONTAINS KEY 'NoSQL';

user_id | user_name | registration
———+——————+————————————————
1006 | Michael Jones | {'Big data': 2017-02-11, 'NoSQL':
2017-01-10}
(1 rows)

Cassandra Development Part 4 is completed.

Cassandra Development
Part 5

Cassandra Cluster Manager

Cassandra Cluster Manager (**CCM**) is a great tool to quickly create and manage a cluster on local server.

The goal of **CCM** is to make it easy to create, manage and remove a small Cassandra cluster on a local server. It is meant for testing a Cassandra cluster.

The following example lists the **CCM** commands to work on Cassandra cluster in shell environment.

(1) Check CCM

Open new shell session.
To check existing ccm, run ccm list command:

$ ccm list

(2) Create new Cassandra Cluster

Using the following ccm command to create cluster with three nodes:

```
$ ccm create new_cluster -v 3.1.1 -n 3
```

Current cluster is now: new_cluster

```
$ ccm list
*new_cluster
```

(3) Populate Cassandra Cluster with three nodes

The following example shows populating Cassandra cluster with three nodes:

```
$ ccm populate -n 3
```

```
$ sudo ifconfig lo0 alias 127.0.0.2
```

```
$ sudo ifconfig lo0 alias 127.0.0.3
```

(4) Start CCM

To start CCM, run the following command:
```
$ ccm start
```

(5) Check CCM Status

```
$ ccm status
```
Cluster: 'new_cluster'
— — — — — — —-
node1: UP
node3: UP
node2: UP

(6) Show CCM Configuration Information

Check node status:

$ ccm node1 show

```
node1: UP
cluster=new_cluster
auto_bootstrap=False
thrift=('127.0.0.1', 9160)
binary=('127.0.0.1', 9042)
storage=('127.0.0.1', 7000)
jmx_port=7100
remote_debug_port=0
byteman_port=0
initial_token=-9223372036854775808
pid=891
```

$ ccm node2 show

```
node2: UP
cluster=new_cluster
auto_bootstrap=False
thrift=('127.0.0.2', 9160)
binary=('127.0.0.2', 9042)
storage=('127.0.0.2', 7000)
jmx_port=7200
remote_debug_port=0
byteman_port=0
initial_token=-3074457345618258603
pid=890
```

$ *ccm node3 show*

node3: UP
cluster=new_cluster
auto_bootstrap=False
thrift=('127.0.0.3', 9160)
binary=('127.0.0.3', 9042)
storage=('127.0.0.3', 7000)
jmx_port=7300
remote_debug_port=0
byteman_port=0
initial_token=3074457345618258602
pid=889

Check CCM status:

$ *ccm node1 ring*

Datacenter: datacenter1
==========
Address Rack Status State Load Owns Token
3074457345618258602
127.0.0.1 rack1 Up Normal 102.98 KB ? -
9223372036854775808
127.0.0.2 rack1 Up Normal 122.09 KB ? -
3074457345618258603
127.0.0.3 rack1 Up Normal 126.97 KB ?
3074457345618258602

(7) Start Cassandra CQLSH mode

$ *ccm node1 cqlsh*

Connected to new_cluster at 127.0.0.1:9042.
[cqlsh 5.0.1 | Cassandra 3.1.1 | CQL spec 3.3.1 | Native protocol v4]
Use HELP for help.
cqlsh>

(8) Create New Keyspace

The following example shows using CQLSH to create new keyspace:

cqlsh> *CREATE KEYSPACE dev WITH replication = {'class': 'SimpleStrategy', 'replication_factor': '3'} AND durable_writes = true;*

cqlsh> *describe keyspaces;*

system_schema system_auth system dev
system_distributed system_traces

(9) Stop CCM

$ *ccm stop*
$ *ccm status*

Cluster: 'new_cluster'
— — — — — — —-
node1: DOWN
node3: DOWN
node2: DOWN

(10) Remove CCM

```
$ ccm remove
$ ccm list
$
```

Cassandra Development Part 5 is completed.

Business Intelligence
(Part 1)

Business intelligence (BI) project deals with large volume of data process. Business intelligence requires not only large volume data storage, but also needs fast speed servers to process business data.

The purpose of Business Intelligence is to support better business decision making. Business intelligence enables business users to perform access and analysis of business information that can be used to help users to obtain current market trends. The information from BI system can help companies to make crucial business decision and improve business productivity.

As the example of business intelligence project this article discusses the following four parts that are often used in business intelligence project to store data in data warehouse.

Part 1. Star Schema

Part 2. Dimension Table Load

Part 3. Fact Table Load

Part 4. Table Partitioning

Part 1. Star Schema

Star schema consists of fact table and dimension tables. Star schema is the most common architecture used as data warehouse implementation and it is also popular model in business intelligence project.

A fact table contains foreign key columns which point to dimension tables and measures which provide numeric facts. A dimension table is usually composed of one or more hierarchies that categorize data, such as products, location, time and customer.

The following chart shows the example of star schema. It consists of sales fact table and four dimension tables: Dim_Date, Dim_Product, Dim_Customer and Dim_Store.

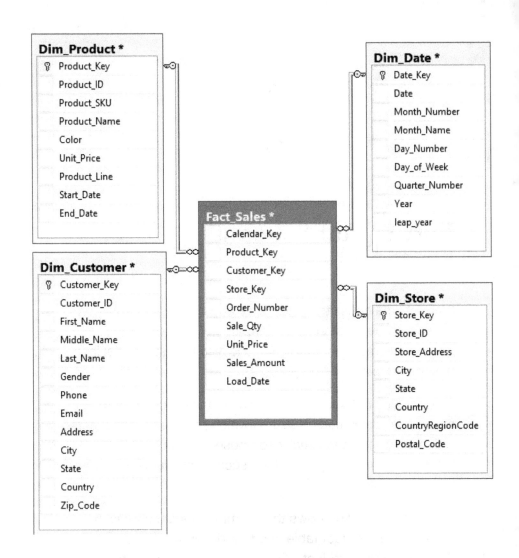

The dimension table structure and example data are listed as the following screenshots.

This is the example of Dim_Product dimension:

Product Key	Product ID	Product SKU	Product Name	Color	Unit Price	Product Line	Start Date	End Date
157	852	TG-W091-S	Women's Tights, S	Black	74.99	S	7/1/2006	6/30/2007
158	853	TG-W091-M	Women's Tights, M	Black	74.99	S	7/1/2006	6/30/2007
159	854	TG-W091-L	Women's Tights, L	Black	74.99	S	7/1/2006	6/30/2007
160	855	SB-M891-S	Men's Bib-Shorts, S	Multi	89.99	S	7/1/2006	6/30/2007
161	856	SB-M891-M	Men's Bib-Shorts, I	Multi	89.99	S	7/1/2006	6/30/2007
162	857	SB-M891-L	Men's Bib-Shorts, I	Multi	89.99	S	7/1/2006	6/30/2007
163	858	GL-H102-S	Half-Finger Gloves	Black	24.49	S	7/1/2006	NULL
164	859	GL-H102-M	Half-Finger Gloves	Black	24.49	S	7/1/2006	NULL
165	860	GL-H102-L	Half-Finger Gloves	Black	24.49	S	7/1/2006	NULL
166	861	GL-F110-S	Full-Finger Gloves,	Black	37.99	M	7/1/2006	6/30/2007
167	862	GL-F110-M	Full-Finger Gloves,	Black	37.99	M	7/1/2006	6/30/2007
168	863	GL-F110-L	Full-Finger Gloves,	Black	37.99	M	7/1/2006	6/30/2007
169	864	VE-C304-S	Classic Vest, S	Blue	63.5	S	7/1/2007	NULL
170	865	VE-C304-M	Classic Vest, M	Blue	63.5	S	7/1/2007	NULL

This is the example of Dim_Date dimension:

Date Key	Date	Month Number	Month Name	Day Number	Day of Week	Quarter Number	Year	Leap Year
20180101	1/1/2018	1	January	1	Monday	1	2018	0
20180102	1/2/2018	1	January	2	Tuesday	1	2018	0
20180103	1/3/2018	1	January	3	Wednesday	1	2018	0
20180104	1/4/2018	1	January	4	Thursday	1	2018	0
20180105	1/5/2018	1	January	5	Friday	1	2018	0
20180106	1/6/2018	1	January	6	Saturday	1	2018	0
20180107	1/7/2018	1	January	7	Sunday	1	2018	0
20180108	1/8/2018	1	January	8	Monday	1	2018	0
20180109	1/9/2018	1	January	9	Tuesday	1	2018	0
20180110	1/10/2018	1	January	10	Wednesday	1	2018	0
20180111	1/11/2018	1	January	11	Thursday	1	2018	0
20180112	1/12/2018	1	January	12	Friday	1	2018	0
20180113	1/13/2018	1	January	13	Saturday	1	2018	0
20180114	1/14/2018	1	January	14	Sunday	1	2018	0
20180115	1/15/2018	1	January	15	Monday	1	2018	0

This is the example of Dim_Store dimension:

Store Key	Store ID	Store Address	City	State	Country	Country RegionCode	Postal Code
16	306	9 Guadalupe Dr.	Burbank	CA	United States	US	91502
17	307	50 Big Canyon Road	Lebanon	OR	United States	US	97355
18	308	65 Park Glen Court	Port Orchard	WA	United States	US	98366
19	309	28 San Marino Ct.	Bellingham	WA	United States	US	98225
20	310	2472 Alexander Place	West Covina	ID	United States	US	83301
21	311	9830 May Way	Mill Valley	MT	United States	US	59715
22	312	1286 Cincerto Circle	Lake Oswego	OR	United States	US	97034
23	313	2141 Delaware Ct.	Downey	TN	United States	US	37501
24	314	218 Fall Creek Road	West Covina	CA	United States	US	91791
25	315	5807 Churchill Dr.	Corvallis	OR	United States	US	97330
26	316	6061 St. Paul Way	Everett	MT	United States	US	98201
27	317	628 Muir Road	Los Angeles	CA	United States	US	90012
28	318	2313 B Southampton Rd	Missoula	MT	United States	US	59801
29	319	137 Lancelot Dr	Phoenix	AZ	United States	US	85004

This is the example of Fact_Sales table:

Calendar Key	Product Key	Customer Key	Store Key	Order Number	Sale Qty	Unit Price	Sales Amount	Load Date
20140102	485	16930	9	SO74277	1	21.98	21.98	6/22/2018 9:05
20140102	467	16930	9	SO74277	2	24.49	48.98	6/22/2018 9:05
20140102	475	27516	9	SO74278	2	69.99	139.98	6/22/2018 9:05
20140102	490	27516	9	SO74278	1	53.99	53.99	6/22/2018 9:05
20140102	477	11115	9	SO74279	5	4.99	24.95	6/22/2018 9:05
20140102	478	11115	9	SO74279	1	9.99	9.99	6/22/2018 9:05
20140102	473	11115	9	SO74279	1	63.5	63.5	6/22/2018 9:05
20140102	484	11467	9	SO74280	4	7.95	31.8	6/22/2018 9:05
20140102	529	13124	9	SO74281	2	3.99	7.98	6/22/2018 9:05
20140102	541	26637	4	SO74282	1	28.99	28.99	6/22/2018 9:05
20140102	530	26637	4	SO74282	1	4.99	4.99	6/22/2018 9:05
20140102	463	26637	4	SO74282	6	24.49	146.94	6/22/2018 9:05
20140102	539	28762	1	SO74283	1	24.99	24.99	6/22/2018 9:05

Star schema used in business intelligence normally have many dimensions. It is not unusually that a star schema contains 15 or more dimensions.

Part 2. Dimension Table Load

This part discusses the data load in dimension table.

Dimension tables in data warehouse are the objects to be loaded and updated before loading any fact data in fact tables.

This part uses Dim_Date dimension as example to show how date dimension data are loaded in the table.

(1) Create Dimension Table

The following T-SQL code is used to create Dim_Date table:

```
CREATE TABLE [dbo].[Dim_Date](
  [Date_Key] [int] NOT NULL,
  [Date] [datetime] NOT NULL,
  [Month_Number] [tinyint] NOT NULL,
  [Month_Name] [varchar](12) NOT NULL,
  [Day_Number] [tinyint] NOT NULL,
  [Day_of_Week] [varchar](12) NOT NULL,
  [Quarter_Number] [int] NOT NULL,
  [Year] [int] NOT NULL,
```

[leap_year] [bit] NULL,
    CONSTRAINT [PK_Dates_Dim_Date] PRIMARY
    KEY CLUSTERED
    (
        [Date_Key] ASC
)
) ON [PRIMARY]

Dim_Date table structure is listed as the following:

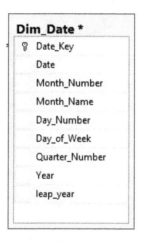

(2) **Populate Dim_Date table**

The following T-SQL code is used to populate the dimension table:

```
DECLARE @StartDate datetime
DECLARE @EndDate datetime
SET @StartDate = '01/01/2004'
SET @EndDate = '12/31/2018'

DECLARE @AddDate datetime
SET @AddDate = @StartDate

WHILE @AddDate <= @EndDate

BEGIN
 INSERT INTO Dim_Date VALUES (
  CAST(CONVERT(varchar, @AddDate, 112) as int),
  @AddDate,
  Month(@AddDate),
  DATENAME(month, @AddDate),
  Day(@AddDate),
  DATENAME(weekday, @AddDate),
  CASE WHEN Month(@AddDate) IN (1, 2, 3) THEN 1
   WHEN Month(@AddDate) IN (4, 5, 6) THEN 2
   WHEN Month(@AddDate) IN (7, 8, 9) THEN 3
   WHEN Month(@AddDate) IN (10, 11, 12) THEN 4
  END,
  Year(@AddDate),
  0
 )
 SET @AddDate = DateAdd(d, 1, @AddDate)
END
```

(3) Update on Leap_Year Column in Dim_Date Table

UPDATE Dim_Date
SET leap_year =
        CASE when ((convert(int,[Year]) % 4 = 0)
        AND (convert(int,[Year]) % 100 != 0
        OR convert(int,[Year]) % 400 = 0))
    then 1
    ELSE 0
END
FROM Dim_Date

After Dim_Date dimension is populated the date is displayed as the following:

Date Key	Date	Month Number	Month Name	Day Number	Day of Week	Quarter Number	Year	Leap Year
20180101	1/1/2018	1	January	1	Monday	1	2018	0
20180102	1/2/2018	1	January	2	Tuesday	1	2018	0
20180103	1/3/2018	1	January	3	Wednesday	1	2018	0
20180104	1/4/2018	1	January	4	Thursday	1	2018	0
20180105	1/5/2018	1	January	5	Friday	1	2018	0
20180106	1/6/2018	1	January	6	Saturday	1	2018	0
20180107	1/7/2018	1	January	7	Sunday	1	2018	0
20180108	1/8/2018	1	January	8	Monday	1	2018	0
20180109	1/9/2018	1	January	9	Tuesday	1	2018	0
20180110	1/10/2018	1	January	10	Wednesday	1	2018	0
20180111	1/11/2018	1	January	11	Thursday	1	2018	0
20180112	1/12/2018	1	January	12	Friday	1	2018	0
20180113	1/13/2018	1	January	13	Saturday	1	2018	0
20180114	1/14/2018	1	January	14	Sunday	1	2018	0
20180115	1/15/2018	1	January	15	Monday	1	2018	0

Part 3. Fact Table Load

Populating fact table in data warehouse includes two steps.

The first step is collecting sales data from OLTP transaction table and loading into a stage database.

The second step is to load fact data from stage area into fact table in data warehouse.

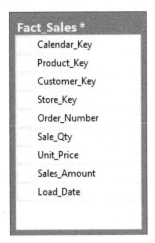

The purpose of this process is to change OLTP natural keys into data warehouse surrogate keys.

The following example shows using SQL query to collect sales data from Sales_Detail table in OLTP system.

(1) Collect New Sales Data from OLTP system into Stage Area

```
INSERT INTO stage.fact_sales_stg
(Date_Key,Product_Key,Customer_Key,Store_Key,Order
_Number,
Order_Qty,Unit_Price,Sales_Amount)
SELECT
ISNULL(d.Date_Key, 0) as Date_Key,
ISNULL(p.Product_Key, 0 ) as Product_Key,
ISNULL(c.Customer_Key, 0) as Customer_Key,
ISNULL(st.Store_Key, 0) as Store_Key,
sd.PurchaseOrderNumber as Order_Number,
sd.OrderQty as Order_Qty,
sd.UnitPrice as Unit_Price,
sd.OrderQty * sd.UnitPrice as Sales_Amount
FROM
stage.Sales_Detail sd
LEFT JOIN DW2014.dbo.Dim_Date d
                ON sd.OrderDate = d.[Date]
LEFT JOIN Dw2014.dbo.Dim_Store st
                ON sd.LocationID = st.Store_ID
LEFT JOIN Dw2014.dbo.Dim_Product p
                ON sd.ProductID = p.Product_ID
LEFT JOIN Dw2014.dbo.Dim_Customer c
                ON sd.CustomerID = c.Customer_ID
WHERE
    sd.OrderDate > '2007-12-31'
```

Data loaded in stage table is listed as the following:

Date_Key	Product_Key	Customer_Key	Store_Key	Order_Number	Order_Qty	Unit_Price	Sales_Amount
20140103	174	11195	5	PO3596133486	7	41.994	293.958
20140103	89	11195	5	PO3596133486	6	1376.994	8261.964
20140103	173	11194	5	PO3596133486	3	41.994	125.982
20140103	287	11194	5	PO3596133486	1	461.694	461.694
20140103	240	11194	5	PO3596133486	1	24.294	24.294
20140103	223	11193	5	PO3596133486	1	158.43	158.43
20140103	53	11193	5	PO3596133486	3	818.7	2456.1
20140103	88	11192	5	PO3596133486	4	1376.994	5507.976
20140103	291	11192	5	PO3596133486	1	112.998	112.998
20140103	85	11192	5	PO3596133486	2	1391.994	2783.988
20140103	210	11191	5	PO3596133486	1	218.454	218.454
20140103	292	11191	5	PO3596133486	2	112.998	225.996
20140103	242	11190	5	PO3596133486	1	48.594	48.594
20140103	289	11190	5	PO3596133486	2	112.998	225.996
20140103	264	11189	7	PO3567173828	3	445.41	1336.23
20140103	198	11189	7	PO3567173828	3	602.346	1807.038

(2) Insert data from stage into fact table fact_Sales

The structure of Fact_Sales listed as the following:

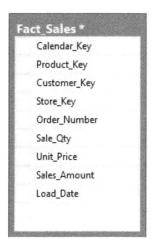

Fact_Sales *
- Calendar_Key
- Product_Key
- Customer_Key
- Store_Key
- Order_Number
- Sale_Qty
- Unit_Price
- Sales_Amount
- Load_Date

Using the following T-SQL code to insert data from stage area into fact table:

```
INSERT INTO DW2014.dbo.Fact_Sales
        (Date_Key,Product_Key,Customer_Key,Store_Key,
        Order_Number,Order_Qty,Unit_Price,Sales_Amount)
SELECT
        Date_Key,Product_Key,Customer_Key,Store_Key,
        Order_Number,Order_Qty,Unit_Price,Sales_Amount
FROM stage.fact_sales_stg
```

(3) Review date in Fact table

After fact data loaded the fact data is displayed as the following:

Calendar Key	Product Key	Customer Key	Store Key	Order Number	Sale Qty	Unit Price	Sales Amount	Load Date
20140102	485	16930	9	SO74277	1	21.98	21.98	6/22/2018 9:05
20140102	467	16930	9	SO74277	2	24.49	48.98	6/22/2018 9:05
20140102	475	27516	9	SO74278	2	69.99	139.98	6/22/2018 9:05
20140102	490	27516	9	SO74278	1	53.99	53.99	6/22/2018 9:05
20140102	477	11115	9	SO74279	5	4.99	24.95	6/22/2018 9:05
20140102	478	11115	9	SO74279	1	9.99	9.99	6/22/2018 9:05
20140102	473	11115	9	SO74279	1	63.5	63.5	6/22/2018 9:05
20140102	484	11467	9	SO74280	4	7.95	31.8	6/22/2018 9:05
20140102	529	13124	9	SO74281	2	3.99	7.98	6/22/2018 9:05
20140102	541	26637	4	SO74282	1	28.99	28.99	6/22/2018 9:05
20140102	530	26637	4	SO74282	1	4.99	4.99	6/22/2018 9:05
20140102	463	26637	4	SO74282	6	24.49	146.94	6/22/2018 9:05
20140102	539	28762	1	SO74283	1	24.99	24.99	6/22/2018 9:05

Part 4. Table Partitioning

Table partitioning in data warehouse is often needed because data warehouse usually consists of large volume data which resides in huge data storage.

Table partitioning brings many benefits in data warehouse. It improves query performance for daily data analysis. Table partitioning can also speed up data loading and data archiving during data warehouse daily activities.

Partitioned table is divides into smaller and more manageable data parts in existing table. Data in a partitioned table is physically stored in different partition groups, so data and index can be easily maintained in the partitions.

The following table partitioning example uses Microsoft SQL Server 2014 as database server. Microsoft T-SQL queries are used in the example.

(1) Review Fact Table

The fact table is called wis_fact_load. The table contains multiple years sales data with sales amount and order data from year 2010 to 2014.

The partial data in table is displayed as the following screenshot:

SalesOrderNumber	OrderQuantity	UnitPrice	SalesAmount	OrderDate	Year_number
SO43706	1	3578.27	3578.27	2010-12-31 00:00:00.000	2010
SO43707	1	3578.27	3578.27	2010-12-31 00:00:00.000	2010
SO43708	1	699.0982	699.0982	2010-12-31 00:00:00.000	2010
SO43709	1	3578.27	3578.27	2010-12-31 00:00:00.000	2010
SO43710	1	3578.27	3578.27	2010-12-31 00:00:00.000	2010
SO43711	1	3578.27	3578.27	2011-01-01 00:00:00.000	2011
SO43712	1	3578.27	3578.27	2011-01-01 00:00:00.000	2011
SO43713	1	3578.27	3578.27	2011-01-02 00:00:00.000	2011
SO43714	1	3578.27	3578.27	2011-01-02 00:00:00.000	2011
SO43715	1	3578.27	3578.27	2011-01-02 00:00:00.000	2011
SO43716	1	3578.27	3578.27	2011-01-02 00:00:00.000	2011
SO43717	1	699.0982	699.0982	2011-01-02 00:00:00.000	2011
SO43718	1	3578.27	3578.27	2011-01-03 00:00:00.000	2011
SO43719	1	3578.27	3578.27	2011-01-03 00:00:00.000	2011

(2) Count the Number of Records by Year

The following T-SQL query count the number of data records by year:

SELECT Year_number, COUNT(*)
as Number_Records
FROM dbo.wis_fact_load
GROUP BY Year_number
ORDER BY Year_number

The following is the result of query output. Year 2013 contains the largest number of records.

Year_number	Number_Records
2010	14
2011	2216
2012	3397
2013	52801
2014	1970

(3) Create Data Files for Partitions

The following T-SQL codes create partition data files by year between 2010 and 2014. The fact data will be allocated in the data files according to the year number in data. The file group is called fact_sales_group.

```
ALTER DATABASE stage_load
ADD FILE
(NAME = sales_2010, FILENAME =
'E:\SQLData\sales_2010.ndf',
 SIZE = 1024MB, FILEGROWTH = 100MB)
TO FILEGROUP fact_sales_group;
GO
ALTER DATABASE stage_load
ADD FILE
(NAME = sales_2011, FILENAME =
'E:\SQLData\sales_2011.ndf',
 SIZE = 1024MB, FILEGROWTH = 100MB)
```

```
TO FILEGROUP fact_sales_group;
GO
ALTER DATABASE stage_load
ADD FILE
(NAME = sales_2012, FILENAME =
'E:\SQLData\sales_2012.ndf',
 SIZE = 1024MB, FILEGROWTH = 100MB)
TO FILEGROUP fact_sales_group;
GO
ALTER DATABASE stage_load
ADD FILE
(NAME = sales_2013, FILENAME =
'E:\SQLData\sales_2013.ndf',
 SIZE = 1024MB, FILEGROWTH = 100MB)
TO FILEGROUP fact_sales_group;
GO
ALTER DATABASE stage_load
ADD FILE
(NAME = sales_2014, FILENAME =
'E:\SQLData\sales_2014.ndf',
 SIZE = 1024MB, FILEGROWTH = 100MB)
TO FILEGROUP fact_sales_group;
GO
```

(4) Create Partition Function

The following T-SQL code is used to create partition function for data between year 2010 and 2014.

```
CREATE PARTITION FUNCTION wis_fact_part_fn(int)
AS
RANGE LEFT FOR VALUES (2010, 2011, 2012, 2013,
2014);
```

Command *"**AS RANGE LEFT**"* makes six partitions:

Partition 1 contains data in year 2010,

Partition 2 contains data in year 2011,

....

Partition 5 contains data in year 2014.

Partition 6 contains data later then year 2014.

(5) Create Partition Schema

The following T-SQL code is used to create partition schema
which calls the partition function created above in step (4):

```
CREATE PARTITION SCHEME
        wis_fact_part_scheme
AS
PARTITION wis_fact_part_fn
ALL TO (fact_sales_group);
```

Output message:

> *Partition scheme 'wis_fact_part_scheme' has been created successfully.*
>
> *'fact_sales_group' is marked as the next used filegroup in partition scheme 'wis_fact_part_scheme'.*

(6) Create Partition Table

Create partition table for fact table which resides on partition scheme wis_fact_part_scheme.

```
CREATE TABLE [dbo].[wis_fact_sales](
 [Fact_Key] int IDENTITY(1,1) NOT NULL,
 [ProductKey] [int] NOT NULL,
 [OrderDateKey] [int] NOT NULL,
 [CustomerKey] [int] NOT NULL,
 [LocationKey] [int] NOT NULL,
 [SalesOrderNumber] [nvarchar](20) NOT NULL,
 [OrderQuantity] [smallint] NOT NULL,
 [UnitPrice] [money] NOT NULL,
 [SalesAmount] [money] NOT NULL,
 [OrderDate] [datetime] NULL,
 [Year_Number] [int] NOT NULL
 CONSTRAINT pk_wis_fact_sales PRIMARY KEY
CLUSTERED
 (Fact_Key, Year_Number)
) ON wis_fact_part_scheme(Year_Number)
```

Here Fact_Key and Year_Number are used as Primary Key.

(7) Load Fact Data into Partitioned Table

The following query load sales data into partitioned table:

```
INSERT INTO [dbo].[wis_fact_sales]
        (ProductKey, OrderDateKey, CustomerKey,
        LocationKey, SalesOrderNumber,
        OrderQuantity, UnitPrice, SalesAmount,
        OrderDate, Year_Number)
SELECT
        ProductKey, OrderDateKey, CustomerKey,
        LocationKey, SalesOrderNumber,
        OrderQuantity, UnitPrice, SalesAmount,
        OrderDate, Year_number
FROM dbo.wis_fact_load
```

(8) Check Partition Results

Run the following SQL query to check partition data:

```
select * from sys.partitions
where object_id=object_id('wis_fact_sales')
```

The output screenshot as the following:

partition_number	hobt_id	rows	
1	72057594088128512	14	
2	72057594088194048	2216	
3	72057594088259584	3397	
4	72057594088325120	52801	
5	72057594088390656	1970	
6	72057594088456192	0	

The output results show that the sales data have been allocated in different partitions according to partition year number.

The number 4 partition contains 52801 records which is year 2013 sales data.